Against the Tl

AGAINST THE THIRD WAY

An Anti-Capitalist Critique

Alex Callinicos

Polity

First published in 2001 by Polity Press
in association with Blackwell Publishers Ltd

Editorial office:
Polity Press
65 Bridge Street
Cambridge CB2 1UR, UK

Marketing and production:
Blackwell Publishers Ltd
108 Cowley Road
Oxford OX4 1JF, UK

Published in the USA by
Blackwell Publishers Inc.
350 Main Street
Malden, MA 02148, USA

A catalogue record for this book is available from the British Library.

Library of Congress Cataloging-in-Publication Data
Callinicos, Alex.
    Against the third way / Alex Callinicos.
        p. cm.
    ISBN 0-7456-2674-2 (HB) — ISBN 0-7456-2675-0 (PB)
    1. International economic relations. 2. Globalization. 3.
Capitalism. 4. Socialism. I. Title.
    HF1359.C345 2001
    337—dc21
                                                    00-012982

Typeset in 11 on 13 pt Sabon
by SetSystems Ltd, Saffron Walden, Essex
Printed and bound in Great Britain by Athenaeum Press Ltd.,
Gateshead, Tyne & Wear
This book is printed on acid-free paper.

Contents

Preface and Acknowledgements

This book is a slight case of biting the hand that feeds one, since it devotes much critical attention to the recent writings of two of Polity's founding editors, Tony Giddens and David Held. In David's case, it is his own fault, since, once again, he encouraged me to write this book. His views are only obliquely targeted here, since he is, like me, a critic of the Third Way; as I try to show in what follows, Third Way ideology can only be properly stated by drawing on the work of theorists who are themselves politically opposed to the Blair–Clinton 'project', even though they rely on some of the same premises that it does. I am in any case grateful to Tony and David for the intellectual generosity that is so characteristic of Polity as a publishing house. Sandra Byatt, Louise Knight, Gill Motley, and Pam Thomas have – not for the first time – smoothed my book's path to publication; I would like to thank all of them, and also Justin Dyer, who copyedited the manuscript.

Sam Ashman, Chris Harman, and three anonymous referees read and commented on this book in draft. I am grateful to all of them, but especially to the author of the last reader's report, which, quite apart from anything else, made me laugh (a rare experience in these circumstances). Welcome though their advice was, I have largely gone my own way in this book: it is offered in a spirit of combat, at a time when the left is beginning to renew itself internationally. This is not a moment to take intellectual prisoners or to compromise with a political project that amounts to the abandonment of any challenge to global capitalism.

Introduction

Approaching the Third Way

The Third Way promises us an escape from the burdens of history. Beyond old polarities that represent the failure of traditional left and right alike, it purports to offer a way forward that captures the best of both traditions. Yet this dialectical transcendence of past errors at the same time constitutes, so it is claimed, the renewal of the left – or rather of the centre-left, as its champions usually prefer to rebaptize the social-democratic tradition.

The Third Way is more than an idea. Apparently given its current usage by the New Democrats who captured the White House under Bill Clinton, it has provided New Labour under Tony Blair with its ideological banner. A somewhat more cautious version, *die neue Mitte* (the new centre), was the watchword of Gerhard Schröder when he led Germany's Social Democrats back to office in the autumn of 1998.[1] Treated with suspicion by other European social democrats, notably the French Socialist Party under Lionel Jospin, the Third Way has nevertheless set the agenda for the moderate left on a European, and indeed a global, scale. Key Third

World figures such as Presidents Kim Dae-jung of South Korea and Fernando Henrique Cardoso of Brazil were quick to jump on the band-wagon.

Supporters of the Third Way are keen to stress these international connections. Clinton, for example, invoked Blair's support to propose a 'third way' between 'those who said government was the enemy' and 'those who said government was the solution' when outlining his social security policy.[2] In April 1999, the American President took time off from waging war against Yugoslavia to host a seminar on the Third Way attended by the German Chancellor and the Prime Ministers of Britain, Italy and the Netherlands. Though Clinton has now departed the White House, the idea of the Third Way has survived his presidency. Indeed, according to some aides, Clinton's role is now to act as 'World President of the Third Way' (though the sleazy manner of his exit from Washington may have put paid to this).

Such impressive sponsorship suggests that it is worth taking the Third Way seriously. But what, precisely, does it stand for? The metaphor derives its content from the two paths not taken, or abandoned, for a third, presumably better route. According to the Third Way's most prominent intellectual exponent, Anthony Giddens, these are, on the one hand, 'old-style social democracy', which had excessive faith in the state, and neo-liberalism, which has put equally misplaced trust in the unregulated market. The Third Way thus lies beyond Old Left and New Right.[3]

Paradoxically the idea has received its strongest institutional support in Britain, the European country whose public culture is most resistant to abstract ideas and to the intellectuals who specialize in articulating them. Here the efforts by New Labour figures to develop an ideological justification for their policies has been met with widespread ridicule, while a media obsessed with the nuances of political intrigue have been quick to document the distaste for the Third Way shown even by some of the most prominent figures in the Blair government.

This cynical response is far from being wholly misjudged.

The fiasco of New Labour's 'ethical' foreign policy, which had hardly been outlined by the new Foreign Secretary, Robin Cook, after the 1997 general election before it succumbed to the powerful Whitehall complex centred on the Ministry of Defence and the Department of Trade and Industry with long-standing interests in selling arms to Third World tyrannies, is a salutary warning to those credulous of vague professions of good intentions. The kind of deflationary tactic suggested by this example does not, however, seem to me sufficient.

The Third Way is not simply associated with some of the most powerful Western governments. It has some formidable intellectual champions. The most notable, Giddens, is a prolific and, with good reason, internationally renowned social theorist. His book *The Third Way* has not simply been taken as a more or less canonical statement of the ideology informing New Labour policy, but has been translated into no less than twenty-five languages.[4] In a more recent book, Giddens has sought to restate the case for the Third Way and to rebut the most common criticism made of it on the left, namely that it is Thatcherism pursued by other means. 'Third way politics is not a continuation of neo-liberalism,' he insists, 'but an alternative political philosophy.'[5] Other leading sociologists such as Ulrich Beck and Manuel Castells have associated themselves with the general enterprise, though usually with considerably greater caution than Giddens. At a further remove, Jürgen Habermas, the leading philosopher of the Western left, has advocated what he calls an 'offensive variant of the Third Way'.[6]

These intellectual credentials suggest that it might be worthwhile trying to establish what content the arguments of the Third Way's proponents have and whether these are valid. Such, at any rate, is the aim of this short book.

Origins

The biggest obstacle facing this enterprise is that, as commentators frequently complain, the formula is so vague and slippery. Winston Churchill famously once called the Labour Prime Minister Ramsay MacDonald a 'boneless wonder'. It is tempting to say the same about the ideology used by MacDonald's latest successor to justify his policies. This is at least partly a consequence of the fact that, as I have already observed, the phrase obtains definite content from the two options that it rejects. Not surprisingly, then, its prehistory lies in very different political quarters from that of the contemporary centre-left.

Norberto Bobbio notes that the formula 'Neither right nor left' was used by the French fascist movement,

> which preceded and influenced Italian Fascism, and mainly consisted of a merger between socialism and nationalism – or, in other words, between a typically left-wing ideology and a typically right-wing ideology. It could equally well have called itself '*Both* right and left', the synthesis of two opposing ideologies, rather than their elimination. The Italian extreme right often uses a formula which removes any remaining doubt about the possible dual choice between rejection and synthesis: 'beyond left and right'. All three formulas represent a third way which can be interpreted as both inclusive and exclusive.[7]

Naturally this is rather an unhappy precedent for a cosmopolitan democrat like Giddens (who is also the author of a book called *Beyond Left and Right*). Perhaps he would be comforted to know that as long ago as 1912 Ramsay MacDonald presented Labourism as 'the third way' between State Socialism and Syndicalism.[8] But a very similar formula is to be found much further to the left. For the American Trotskyist Max Shachtman, the 'third camp' represented those forces capable of achieving greater democracy and social progress in a world dominated by two rival imperialist power-complexes – first the Western liberal democracies and Nazi Germany, later the two superpower blocs during the Cold War.[9] Shachtman himself eventually succumbed to Cold War liberalism, but it was not uncommon for the New Left that began to emerge after 1956 to define itself, not explicitly as a Third Way, but nevertheless as a break from the two dominant traditions on the left. Peter Sedgewick wrote at the end of the 1960s:

> Winding up the last of the volumes that comprised his *History of Socialist Thought*, the late G. D. H. Cole added, shortly before his death in 1959, a short personal credo: 'I am neither a Communist nor a Social Democrat, because I regard both as creeds of centralization and bureaucracy.' Such a statement, at the time it was written and for decades previously, could be no more than a solitary confession of faith. . . . To be a Socialist – and at the same time to be out of sympathy with the ideologies offered within the Communist and the Social-Democratic parties – was an extraordinary position, requiring a special explanation. Today, Cole's declaration could be inscribed as a banner to which tens of thousands of young Socialists, not only in Britain but in France, in Germany, in the United States, would willingly rally.[10]

The political meaning of the 1960s was precisely the temporary breakdown of the hold of Stalinist and social-democratic orthodoxies on substantial radicalized minorities in the Western liberal democracies. For those participating in the movements of the time, both the main alternatives on the left – either the progressive reform of liberal capitalism or resort to the alternative model supposedly offered by 'existing socialism' in the Soviet Union and its satellites – represented, in fact, options for the status quo.[11] Here, of course, lies a fundamental difference from the conjuncture in which the Third Way in its current version took shape.

Today, 'existing socialism' no longer exists, nor does the Soviet Union itself. Giddens explicitly links the rise of the Third Way to '[t]he death of socialism'. His account of what he means by socialism is extremely vague. Thus he writes: 'The notion that capitalism can be humanized through socialist economic management gives socialism whatever hard edge it possesses.'[12] Left-wing social democrats, as well as revolutionary socialists and Stalinists, would all agree that capitalism cannot be humanized, though they would disagree about how and with what it should be replaced. Giddens also fails to specify what he means by 'socialist economic management', but it is nevertheless clear enough that for him both Stalinism and traditional social democracy shared in common the idea that a necessary condition for overcoming the injustices and dysfunctions of capitalism was the establishment of an economic system steered by the state, whether by means of centralized planning or Keynesian demand management.

Thus the first of the two alternatives that the Third Way seeks to transcend has at its core what one might call 'economic statism'. Giddens comprehensively ignores the fact that many versions of socialism do not seek to transcend capitalism by increasing the power of the state precisely because such a solution would simply expand what Cole calls 'centralization and bureaucracy'. Marx, for example, would have dismissed the expression 'state socialism' – regularly used by Giddens in his earlier theoretical writings – as an oxymoron. 'Freedom consists in converting the state from an organ superimposed on society into one completely subordinate to it,' he wrote in the 'Critique of the Gotha Programme'.[13]

Socialism in the sense of economic statism was compromised not simply by the collapse of Stalinism in the East, but also by the crisis of the Keynesian welfare state since the 1970s. Giddens explains:

> In hindsight, we can be fairly clear why the Soviet Union, far from surpassing the US, fell dramatically behind it, and why social democracy encountered its own crises. The economic theory of socialism was always inadequate, underestimating the capacity of capitalism to innovate, adapt and generate increasing productivity. Socialism also failed to grasp the significance of markets as informational devices, providing essential data for buyers and sellers. These inadequacies only became fully revealed with intensifying processes of globalization and technological change from the early 1970s onwards.[14]

Globalization on this account exposed the flaws inherent in economic statism. Here we encounter an asymmetry between the alternatives rejected by the Third Way. Socialism (in the restricted meaning that Giddens gives the word) is dead. But neo-liberalism, the second option, is very much alive. The policies constituting the 'Washington consensus' enforced internationally by the US Treasury and the International Monetary Fund – privatization, deregulation, fiscal and monetary stability – were pioneered by Ronald Reagan and Margaret Thatcher in the 1980s. Though the New Right subsequently lost office in the major liberal democracies, its influence remains considerable, as is indicated by the strength of various right-wing currents within the Republican Party which recaptured the White House in December 2000, and by the effective takeover of the British Conservative Party by the forces of Thatcherite Euroscepticism that were always a minority in the cabinets presided over by their heroine. Giddens may claim that 'neo-liberalism is in trouble', but only a fool would write it off.[15]

Indeed, many would argue that the hegemony of neo-liberalism is demonstrated precisely by the fact that its policies survived the electoral defeat of the parties that inaugurated it. The point is made with particular trenchancy by Perry Anderson:

> The winning formula to seal the victory of the market is not to attack, but to preserve the placebo of a compassionate public authority, extolling the compatibility of competition with solidarity. The hard core of government policies remains further pursuit of the Reagan–Thatcher legacy, on occasion with measures their predecessors did not dare enact: welfare reform in the US, student fees in the UK. But it is now carefully surrounded with subsidiary concessions and softer rhetoric. The effect of this combination, currently being diffused throughout Europe, is to suppress the conflictual potential of the pioneering regimes of the radical right, and kill off opposition to neo-liberal hegemony more completely. One might say that, by definition, TINA [Mrs Thatcher's slogan 'There is no alternative'] only acquires full force once an

alternative regime demonstrates that there are truly no alternative policies. For the quietus to European social democracy or the memory of the New Deal to be consummated, governments of the Centre-Left were indispensable. In this sense, adapting Lenin's maxim that 'the democratic republic is the ideal political shell of capitalism', we could say that the Third Way is the best ideological shell of neo-liberalism today.[16]

Targeting New Labour

Anderson's analysis sets the agenda for any critical assessment of the Third Way. Is it more than an 'ideological shell of neo-liberalism'? Giddens insists that it is, but some of his own pronouncements suggest otherwise. Thus he comments on the idea

> that the left is defined by its concern with the dangers of [the] market, whose excesses need constantly to be reined back by the state. Today, however, this idea has become archaic. The left has to get comfortable with markets, with the role of business in the creation of wealth, and [sic] the fact that private capital is essential for social investment.[17]

Similarly, Gordon Brown, British Chancellor of the Exchequer, not long ago declared 'Labour – the party of enterprise'.[18] But, if all is hunky-dory with capitalism, how *does* the left define itself? The standard New Labour answer is it does so by its values. Handed down from the past, these socialist values remain unaltered, even though the economic and political context has changed, and therefore the policies required to realize them need also to change. Thus Blair and Schröder declare in a key policy statement:

> Fairness and social justice, liberty and equality of opportunity, solidarity and responsibility to others – these values are timeless. Social democracy will never sacrifice them. To make these values relevant to today's world requires realistic

and forward-looking policies capable of meeting the challenges of the 21st century. Modernization is about adapting to conditions that have objectively changed, and not reacting to polls.[19]

Socialism in the sense of a state-steered economic system may be dead, but it survives as a set of values. This way of putting it has at least the advantage of offering some kind of bench-mark by which Third Way administrations can be judged, though (as we shall see) considerable care has to be taken in precisely specifying the normative concepts and principles constituting the values in question.[20] The difficulty is compounded by the ambiguity of the expression 'the Third Way' itself, since significantly different political approaches are encompassed under it. Thus Giddens cites a German study that

> distinguishes four different 'third ways' in Europe. One is the 'market-oriented' approach taken by New Labour. The Dutch approach is 'market- and consensus-oriented'. Sweden is treading the path of the 'reformed welfare state', retaining a good deal of continuity with the past. Continuity of development is also apparent in France, which is sticking to the 'state-led way'.[21]

This seems to stretch the meaning of the formula till it has lost any content whatever. Thus, to take the French case, far from abandoning the ideal of a state-steered economic system, Jospin insists that '[t]he State must provide itself with new instruments of regulation adapted to the reality of the capitalism of today.'[22] He told the Socialist International in November 1999: 'We must . . . rediscover what is useful in the Marxist method: the critical analysis of social realities and thus of capitalism. We must continue to think capitalism, in order to contest it, master it and reform it.'[23] This seems like an example of precisely the kind of 'archaic' thinking denounced by Giddens. It is true that the practice of Jospin's 'plural left' government has been much closer to that of its British and German counterparts than its rhetoric might suggest. Nevertheless, there remains a significant difference between a social-democratic government that follows the time-honoured pattern of managing capitalism while occasionally criticizing it and one that glories in the fact that it is 'comfortable with markets'.

The main focus of my argument will therefore be provided by the theory and practice of New Labour in Britain. There seem to be two particular reasons for doing so. First of all, Blair himself and associates such as Giddens have sought quite aggressively to redefine European social democracy ideologically in terms of their understanding of the Third Way. Other versions – for example, as set out in *The Politics of the New Centre*, by Schröder's former spin-doctor, Bodo Hombach – are more cautious statements of the British argument. Secondly, a British government with the kind of majority in the House of Commons that Blair enjoyed after May 1997 was uniquely well placed in the main liberal democracies actually to implement its policies.

The case of New Labour thus offers an opportunity to analyse this purported renewal of social democracy in a chemically pure form. Blair's and Brown's speeches, plus the writings of Giddens and other New Labour intellectuals such as Charles Leadbeater, provide my main sources for Third Way doctrine. As will become clear, there are important differences within even this very narrow group. Giddens, for example, is considerably more radical in his approach to financial markets than are Blair and Brown, and both he and Leadbeater reveal marked reservations about the 'communitarian' dimension of New Labour ideology.

From a practical political view, the endemic conflicts between Blair and Brown and their respective retinues are, of course, much more significant.[24] But these are driven not by principled disagreements, but by ambition and hatred. (In this respect at least, New Labour is thoroughly Old Labour; when someone told one of the giants of the postwar Attlee government, Ernest Bevin, that another, Herbert Morrison, was his own worst enemy, Bevin muttered: 'Not while I'm alive, he's not.') Brown, despite the care with which he cultivates his connections with Labour traditionalists, and the comparative rarity of his references to the Third Way, is the chief architect of the Blair government's economic and social policies, and his strategy will accordingly receive particular attention in chapter 2.

It would, however, be provincial to focus exclusively on Britain. The experience of the Clinton administration in the United States is particularly important. Not simply did it provide an important model for New Labour, but a crucial dimension of Third Way ideology concerns foreign policy, and more particularly 'the doctrine of the international community' licensing unlimited 'humanitarian intervention' by the Western powers that Blair unveiled in April 1999. Of course, when it comes to translating such professions of what Ulrich Beck has called 'military humanism' into reality, it is the White House that, quite literally, calls the shots. I shall also touch on (though no more) the debate as it has developed in Germany: the joint statement by Blair and Schröder (written in fact by Hombach and his British counterpart, Peter Mandelson) that I have already cited is an important statement of Third Way doctrine.[25]

It cannot, however, be stressed sufficiently that Blair has operated in a socio-political context that is, in one crucial respect, qualitatively more favourable, than that facing Schröder, Jospin or indeed any other European social-democratic leader. Blair has been able to benefit from the achievements of Thatcherism for the business class, not so much in restructuring the British economy as in humbling the British labour movement. Above all, the defeat of the 1984–5 miners' strike severely weakened a trade union movement that had, for much of the previous generation, experienced a steady increase in its economic and social strength.[26]

This historic defeat for organized labour made possible Blair's ascent to the party leadership in the first place; it has also greatly increased his room for manoeuvre in office. Schröder must, by contrast, deal with a labour movement that has not experienced in the post-war period the kind of shock assault that Thatcher launched during the 1980s;

Jospin's more radical rhetoric reflects, in part, the necessity of adapting to the mood of a French working class whose confidence and militancy have been greatly enhanced by the great public sector strikes of November–December 1995. The highly specific constellation of class forces in post-Thatcher Britain underlies and helps to explain the exemplary role played by New Labour in seeking to redefine the nature of social democracy.

It remains for me to outline the general course of my argument. We have already encountered the standard Third Way *topos* – traditional values in a changing world. As Blair puts it, '[t]he resolution of this conflict [i.e. that between tradition and modernity] lies in applying traditional values to the modern world; to leave outdated attitudes behind; but re-discover the essence of traditional values and then let them guide us in managing change.'[27] The interrelationship between ethico-political values and socio-economic change thus constitutes the grid through which proponents of the Third Way view the world.

At one term of the relationship – that of change – is to be found the idea of globalization, understood broadly to encompass the greater integration of the world economically, politically and culturally. The actual portrayal of globalization in Third Way texts is, as we shall see, ambivalent. Sometimes it is depicted as destructive, at other times liberating; to some extent the differing evaluations vary with the dimension of globalization under discussion – thus, on the whole, greater economic integration tends to be regarded as more threatening than political globalization. In chapter 1 I consider the arguments raised by economic globalization. I also examine some of the claims about what is variously called 'informational capitalism' · and the 'knowledge economy'.

I begin to consider the other term of the relationship – timeless values – in chapter 2. Here I am concerned particularly with the role played by the concepts of equality and community in the Third Way. This will allow me to discuss more concretely New Labour economic and social policies, particularly with respect to the extent to which they can be regarded (as their defenders claim) as egalitarian, and (as their critics often contend) as authoritarian. I address the international dimension of Third Way ethics in chapter 3. This involves going well beyond the pronouncements of politicians and ideologues to examine the analysis required to support these pronouncements – namely, that a global political order is emerging that is progressively transcending the rivalries of nation-states and the strategies of the Great Powers.

It will become particularly clear in this chapter what is true of this book more generally – that the arguments put forward by proponents of the Third Way depend, if they are to have any plausibility, on the much more substantial work of intellectuals who may have little directly to do with Blair or Clinton and their courts and may even be highly critical of New Labour and its counterparts elsewhere. But it seems to me an elementary requirement of any serious critique that it should consider its opponents' arguments where they are strongest – even if, as in this case, it requires conscripting others' ideas to shore up these arguments.

Finally, in chapter 4, I consider left alternatives, starting with more radical versions of the Third Way. In doing so I seek also to outline some basic elements of an anti-capitalist position appropriate to the world in which we now live. This should underline what the title of this book makes clear, that I have written a critique of the Third Way from an anti-capitalist perspective. This will come as little surprise to those familiar with any of my other work. But the fact that a long-standing commitment to the revolutionary Marxist tradition predisposes me against the Third Way does not, I hope, make this book a simple parade of prejudices (though I am sure plenty are, consciously or unconsciously, on show).

Unlike many critics who simply dismiss Third Way ideology as superficial drivel, I have tried to take it seriously in its own terms. Even where its proponents' arguments are thin and weak, as is very often the case, they touch on genuinely important issues, most notably concerning the nature of economic and political globalization. These questions are certainly worth clarifying, even though I believe the correct answers offer little comfort to New Labour and its like. To that extent this book should be of interest even to those already sure whether they stand for or against the Third Way.

For some the position from which I have written this critique is simply impossible. History has definitively spoken in favour of capitalism. Jeffrey Isaac writes in support of Giddens: 'given the history that we have inherited and the world that human beings have created, there exists no credible wholesale alternative to capitalism.'[28] Much, of course, depends on the weight we give to those adjectives 'credible' and 'wholesale'. In the social world the idea of the possible is ambivalent between what is really possible – given the structure of that world and of its physical environment – and what is perceived to be possible. Often the former is wider than the latter. In one of the many paradoxes thrown up by world history during the twentieth century, the over-throw of the Stalinist regimes at the end of the 1980s, which showed that the scope for collective political action was much wider than certainly most experts had previously believed, led to a contraction in our sense of the socially possible. Most people came to accept that 'there exists no credible wholesale alternative to capitalism'.

But this state of affairs is beginning to change. The experience over the past two decades of increasingly unrestrained and globalized capitalism has begun to generate a new and powerful revolt against our corporation-governed, commodified world. This revolt will stimulate a renewed search for alternatives to capitalism. This book is a contribution to this new anti-capitalist movement.

1

Masters of the Universe

1.1 The globalization debate

Joe Klein in his *roman à clef Primary Colors* portrays a lightly disguised Bill Clinton addressing a blue-collar audience during the 1992 New Hampshire primary campaign:

> No politician can bring these shipyard jobs back. Or make your union strong again. No politician can make it be the way it used to be. Because we're living in a new world now, a world without borders – economically, that is. Guy can push a button in New York and move a billion dollars to Tokyo before you blink an eye. We've got a world market now.[1]

Here, then, is the central thesis of globalization succinctly outlined. Global economic integration, most evident with respect to financial markets, has radically undermined the autonomy of nation-states, producing 'a world without borders'. There are more ambitious definitions of globalization – thus David Held, Anthony McGrew and their co-authors in the most systematic study of the subject to date view it in very broad terms: 'Globalization may be thought of initially as the widening, deepening and speeding up of worldwide interconnectedness in all aspects of contemporary social life, from the cultural to the criminal, the financial to the spiritual.'[2]

Yet the real bite in the debate about globalization comes from the political consequences that are inferred from what is taken to be the fact of greater international economic integration. It is, for advocates of the Third Way, economic globalization that has rendered obsolete the statism of the Old Left, whether Stalinist or social-democratic. Soon after he became Labour leader Tony Blair spelled this out. He declared in his 1995 Mais lecture that 'the determining context of economic policy is the new global market', and that therefore 'the room for manoeuvre of any government in Britain is already heavily circumscribed.'[3]

This is a reading of globalization that stresses its negative consequences – the respects in which it narrows the choices open to national policy-makers. In a more recent lecture, Blair also highlights the downside of globalization:

> Globalization has brought us economic progress and material well-being. But it also brings fear in its wake. Children offered drugs in the school playground; who grow up sexually at a speed I for one find frightening; parents who struggle in the daily grind of earning a living, raising a family, often with both parents working, looking after elderly relatives; a world where one in three marriages end in divorce; where jobs can come and go because of a decision in a boardroom thousands of miles away; where ties of family, locality and country seem under constant pressure and threat.[4]

Blair's ambivalence about globalization in part reflects the neo-conservative dimension of Third Way thinking, which I discuss at more length in §2.3 below. His remarks also illustrate the tendency in current debates to attribute *all* contemporary social change to globalization. Giddens' 1999 Reith Lectures are an egregious example of this tendency, though this breezy survey of a 'runaway world' is more concerned to highlight the upside of globalization. Thus the transformation of family structures and the associated pressures for equality for women are 'a truly global revolution' that arises (though exactly how is never specified) from globalization. Other beneficent changes also spring from the same source. 'Globalization not only pulls upwards, but also pushes downwards, creating new pressures for local autonomy. . . . Globalization is the reason for the revival of local cultural identities in different parts of the world. . . .' And so on.[5]

In his previous career as a social theorist, Giddens championed explanatory pluralism against what he claimed was Marxism's class reductionism; today, however, his accounts of the social world are relentlessly monolithic in their reduction of social phenomena to the consequences of globalization. They also fail to engage with the considerable debate that has developed over globalization. Giddens acknowledges, but dismisses with little or no argument, the criticisms of sceptics about the more extreme claims made for globalization, who, he says, 'tend to be on the political left, especially the old left'.[6]

But this is nonsense. Sceptics about globalization are to be found throughout the political spectrum, from the free-market right to the revolutionary left. They embrace supporters of very different research programmes – thus, alongside the Marxist political economist Chris Harman we find Kenneth Waltz, doyen of the Realist school of international relations theory, and the Weberian historical sociologist Michael Mann.[7] Moreover, any honest account of those whom Giddens calls the 'radicals' – those who believe that global economic integration is abolishing national differences – would have to give particular credit to the pioneering work of Marxists. During the 1980s Nigel Harris developed one of the first rigorous accounts of economic globalization; Fredric Jameson's celebrated interpretation of postmodernism – also formulated during the 1980s and recently embraced by Perry Anderson – treats it as the cultural correlate of a new, 'multinational' phase of capitalist development.[8]

In their much more careful treatment of globalization Held, McGrew and their collaborators acknowledge that 'none of the great traditions of social enquiry – liberal, conservative and Marxist – has an agreed perspective on globalization as a socio-economic phenomenon.' They treat the debate as occurring between three camps – 'hyperglobalizers', who proclaim the obsolescence of the nation-state, 'sceptics', such as Paul Hirst and Graeme Thompson, who 'argue that globalization is essentially a myth which conceals the reality of an international economy increasingly segmented into three major regional blocs in which national governments remain very powerful', and 'transformationalists', for whom 'contemporary patterns of globalization are conceived as historically unprecedented such that states and societies are experiencing a process of profound change as they try to adapt to a more interconnected but highly uncertain world'.[9]

Held, McGrew and their collaborators also argue that globalization should be seen as a complex, multi-dimensional process rather than a primarily economic phenomenon. They suggest that it should be conceptualized as '*a process (or set of processes) which embodies a transformation in the spatial organization of social relations and transactions – assessed in terms of their extensity, intensity, velocity and impact – generating transcontinental or interregional flows and networks of activity, interaction, and exercise of power*'.[10] Thus understood, globalization must be seen as a trans-historical phenomenon taking different 'historical forms' from pre-modern times to the present.

Held, McGrew and their colleagues are careful to stress that increases in globalization are the contingent outcomes of an irreducible plurality of causes. They insist that 'globalization as a historical process cannot be characterized by an evolutionary logic or an emergent telos.'[11] And they present their case in a scholarly and rigorous fashion. Nevertheless, the general effect of the way they conceptualize globalization is to prejudge the argument against the sceptics. To portray globalization as a trans-historical process only whose contingent forms vary is to settle the debate: globalization is a reality – the only issue concerns the precise modalities of its historical evolution. Moreover, the classification of the debate involves a familiar rhetorical device: by distinguishing the wilder proponents of globalization from the more moderate 'transformationalists', Held, McGrew and their collaborators allow the latter (among whom they include Giddens) to emerge as the authors of a dialectical synthesis that overcomes the errors but incorporates the elements of truth in the cases put by 'hyperglobalizers' and 'sceptics'.

A much more useful contrast would seem to me to be that between boosters and critics. Particularly as a result of the long economic boom experienced by the United States during the 1990s, hype about the future of world capitalism has become a chronic feature of policy and academic debates. The transformation of Alan Greenspan, the hitherto cautious chairman of the US Federal Reserve Board, into a praise-singer for America's 'New Economy' is a case in point. Such hype is characteristic of stock market booms, as those familiar with the history of Wall Street before the October 1929 crash will know. The apparently ceaseless drivel about dot-com companies and e-commerce pumped out even by 'quality' media before this sector of the market embarrassingly crashed in the spring of 2000 is an indication that history may be set to repeat itself.[12]

In any case, those doubtful about the claims that American (and potentially world) capitalism has broken free of past constraints and can expand indefinitely into the future include not merely the usual Marxist suspects, but also, as we shall see, more orthodox economists such as Robert Gordon, Wynne Godley and Bill Martin. This division between boosters and critics cuts across views over globalization. It is perfectly coherent to believe both that global economic integration has qualitatively increased over the past generation and that the probable outcome will be greater rather than less economic instability. (Such, roughly, is my own view.) I think it is a more interesting division than however one wants to classify the parties to the debate on globalization because it seems to me that the main intellectual danger at present is that critical thinking will be engulfed in the deluge of hype about the 'New Economy'.

Boosterism and critical thinking may co-exist in the same writer's work. The Downing Street adviser Charles Leadbeater is a particularly striking case of more or less undiluted boosterism; in Giddens' more recent writing boosterism threatens to overwhelm serious social thought. But others represent more unstable combinations. Thus in Manuel Castells' monumental three-volume study *The Information Age* serious analysis wars with the uncritical celebration of what he calls 'informational capitalism'. I discuss some of his and Leadbeater's claims in §1.3 below.

In what follows I concentrate on the extent and implications of economic globalization, even though Held, McGrew and their collaborators condemn such an approach as 'economistic'.[13] My reason for doing so is that, as I have already noted, this is the critical issue for theorists of the Third Way in differentiating their approach from that of the Old Left. I return to the claims made for political globalization in chapter 3.

1.2   The limits of politics

For the point of view of left strategy, the debate on globalization focuses on two key questions:

1   Has there been a qualitative increase in global economic integration over the past century?
2   If the answer to 1 is 'Yes', does this mean that political action is incapable of controlling, let alone transforming global capitalism?

With respect to Question 1, a century may seem like a long time. It is, however, essential to pose the issue in such a long historical perspective, given the argument of key sceptics, notably Hirst and Thompson. They argue that the level of global economic integration – measured in particular by the dependence of leading economies on foreign trade and the functioning of international financial markets – was comparable at the end of the twentieth century to what it had been before the First World War. Our contemporary sense of living in a globalizing economy derives to a large extent from the fact that, during the era of crisis between 1914 and 1945, the world market fragmented into autarkic economic blocs, leading to a partial retreat from the levels of international integration attained before 1914. The 'globalization' of the past generation has thus been largely a return to the more integrated world economy that prevailed during the *Belle Époque*.[14] Moreover, far from being genuinely global, foreign direct investment and international trade are concentrated in the 'Triad' of advanced capitalist countries (North America, the European Union and Japan), while the assets, sales and output of the multinational corporations (MNCs) that are the main agents of this process are predominantly in their home economies rather than spread around the world.[15]

In response, Held, McGrew and their co-authors point out that, in both absolute terms and relative to world output, international trade has reached unprecedented levels. While they concede that net international capital flows are lower than in the pre-1914 era, they insist that 'the significance of unprecedented gross capital flows and high capital mobility today cannot be discounted so readily.' They also argue that a global system of production is emerging: 'Although economic globalization is often understood simply as the spread of global markets, the growth of MNCs and global production networks represents something rather different: the growing transnational organization of production and distribution among firms instead of through markets.'[16]

Thus carefully stated, the rational kernel in the claims made for economic globalization is, on the one hand, the emergence of highly integrated and mobile financial markets and, on the other, the tendency for the production and distribution of commodities to be organized across national frontiers by MNCs and their satellites (the expansion of international trade is, as Held, McGrew and their co-authors stress, inseparable from this latter tendency). Harman points to the error in Hirst's and Thompson's over-reliance on quantitative comparisons:

> The fact that *levels* of foreign trade and foreign investment were higher in 1914 than today does not in fact prove that nothing has changed with regard to the *organization* of production. The same billion pounds of total investment might represent investment in 100 factories competing with each other, or it might represent investment in a group of factories each carrying through different parts of a single productive process.[17]

This weakness in Hirst's and Thompson's argument does not, however, imply that MNCs are genuinely 'footloose' corporations capable of detaching themselves from any national bases. As Harman stresses, foreign direct investment frequently takes the form of the so-called 'Toyota model', where an MNC does not simply establish a foreign subsidiary but develops a network of local suppliers to provide its plant with components and other inputs. The result is a relationship of mutual interdependence, in which, of course, the suppliers are vulnerable to pressures from the foreign company (as is illustrated by the recent demands made by British-based car multinationals that their local suppliers invoice their goods in cheap euros rather than expensive pounds); at the same time, the subsidiary management is likely to perceive its interests as interwoven with those of its suppliers and to couch its political demands directed at the host government in terms that reflect these common interests. Tearing up this delicate web of relationships by shutting the subsidiary down is likely to be a high-cost decision (though, of course, one that is sometimes taken nevertheless, as is shown by the recent wave of closures of MNC branch plants in Britain).[18]

Finally, such economic globalization as has occurred has depended on state intervention. The point is made quite forcefully by Castells, who is frequently cited by Third Way ideologues such as Giddens and Leadbeater in support of their view of globalization. Indeed Castells argues that economic globalization 'was made possible, and, by and large induced, by deliberate government policies. The global economy was not created by markets, but by the interaction between markets and governments and international financial institutions acting on behalf of markets – or of their notion of what markets ought to be.' According to Castells, three state policies – deregulation, trade liberalization and privatization – 'created the foundations for globalization'. Consequently 'the global economy was politically constituted.'[19] From a longer term perspective this should be hardly surprising. Karl Polanyi famously argued that, far from corresponding to the requirements of human nature, the formation of markets in labour, land and money required the large-scale state-directed reconstruction of European society.[20] What we are seeing today is a similar process on a world scale, as Western governments, acting through agencies such as the IMF and the World Trade Organization, seek to remove national barriers to neo-liberal policies.

So the answer to Question 1 is a qualified 'Yes'. There has been a qualitative increase in global economic integration. What about Question 2: has the scope for political action been so reduced that we must abandon any hope of controlling or transforming capitalism?

Certainly a sense of the narrowed scope for political action is widely felt. One striking example is offered by the political author of the Third Way himself, Bill Clinton. In his account of Clinton's first year in the White House, Bob Woodward describes a meeting in Little Rock on 7 January 1993, shortly before the new President took his oath of office. Alan Blinder and other economists explained to Clinton that his most urgent priority was not to implement the modest platform of reforms on which he had been elected, but to cut the federal budget by $140 billion in an effort to persuade the then very nervous bond markets and the Federal Reserve Board to let interest rates fall:

At the president-elect's end of the table, Clinton's face turned red with anger and disbelief. 'You mean to tell me that the success of the program and my re-election hinges on the Federal Reserve and a bunch of fucking bond dealers?' He responded.

Nods from the end of the table. Not a dissent.

Clinton, it seemed to Blinder, perceived at that moment how much his fate was passing into the hands of the unelected Alan Greenspan and the bond market.[21]

Further down the line, at a White House meeting on 7 April 1993, Clinton raged at the consequences of this strategy:

'Where are all the Democrats?' Clinton bellowed. 'I hope you're all aware we're Eisenhower Republicans,' he said, his voice dripping with sarcasm. 'We're Eisenhower Republicans here, and we're fighting the Reagan Republicans. We stand for lower deficits and free trade and the bond market. Isn't that great? . . . We must have something for the common man. . . . At least we'll have health care to give them, if we can't give them anything else,' he added.[22]

In the event, of course, health care reform was one of the many casualties of Clinton's first term. Considering this scene in the aftermath of the President's impeachment trial, Christopher Hitchens commented, with characteristic lack of charity, but deadly accuracy: 'The Republicanism of Clinton's presidency has not, in fact, risen to the Eisenhower level. He has entrusted policy to much more extreme Republicans like Alan Greenspan and Dick Morris, without manifesting any of the old general's robust suspicion of the military-industrial complex.'[23]

Dick Morris is the Republican political consultant who advised Clinton on how to recover his political fortunes after the defeat of health care reform and the clean sweep made by the Republican right under Newt Gingrich in the 1994 mid-term elections. It was Morris who devised the strategy of 'triangulation' – stealing the Republicans' clothes in order to hang on to the White House in 1996 – whose most odious consequence was Clinton's signature of the welfare 'reform' bill. Yet another anecdote – this time told by Robert Reich, Labor Secretary in Clinton's first term – captures the spirit that informed this strategy:

> 'You've got to understand,' Morris explained to me one day in the main corridor of the West Wing, when I was on one of my forays to find the loop. 'Clinton tacks to the right when the wind is blowing right. He tacks to the left when it's blowing left. Now it's blowing right, so that's where he's heading. But he always knows his ultimate destination.'
> 'Where's *that*, Dick?' I asked him.
> 'Back to the White House for another four years,' he said, without so much as a smile.[24]

Reich was the closest thing to a European social democrat in Clinton's first cabinet. His strategy of seeking simultaneously to increase the competitiveness of the US economy and reduce social inequality through public investment in improved education and training was an important influence on New Labour economic policy as it developed under Gordon Brown (see §2.2 below). Yet his memoir of his time as Labor Secretary wittily but despairingly records the remorseless widening of social divisions while Clinton steadily tacked to the right. Nearly four years after a sadder (and perhaps wiser) Reich left Washington, Robert Pollin offered this damning appraisal of Clinton's economic record through the 1990s: 'Clinton's administration has essentially been defined by across-the-board reductions in government spending, virtually unqualified enthusiasm for free trade, deregulation of financial markets, and only tepid, inconsistent efforts to regulate labour markets.'[25]

The interesting thing about the scenes evoked by Woodward is that they suggest that this outcome was not actually intended by Clinton, and that he subjectively experienced his shift in this direction – motivated, of course, by the ever-present concern to win re-election, but also under the structural pressures represented by 'the Federal Reserve and a bunch of fucking bond dealers' – as a defeat. In consequence, as Castells observes, '[t]he Clinton administration was in fact the true political globalizer' – defending the Washington consensus against all comers, overcoming bitter Democratic resistance to push the North American Free Trade Agreement through the Congress, negotiating the establishment of the World Trade Organization.[26]

If there is anything to this view of Clinton's evolution, then it invites two comments. First, it contrasts strikingly with New Labour's entry into office. Far from bashing their heads on the structural constraints imposed by global capital, Blair and Brown sought to anticipate the demands of big business – first by adopting Tory spending targets in January 1997 and then, on taking office that May, by surrendering control of interest rates to the Bank of England. These self-denying ordinances may have reflected the bitter experience of Labour governments in the 1960s and 1970s, but they suggest the surprising thought that there was a brief moment at the start of his administration when Clinton was to the *left* of New Labour, at least at the equivalent point in their evolution.[27]

Secondly, as mention of past Labour governments suggests, this is a familiar story. The pathos of Clinton raging at his lost programmes recalls that of other political leaders. It is reminiscent, for example, of Harold Wilson's famous description of his confrontation with Lord Cromer, the Governor of the Bank of England, when the latter demanded cuts in public spending in order to maintain confidence in sterling after Labour's election victory in October 1964:

> Not for the first time, I said that we had now reached the situation where a newly elected Government with a mandate from the people was being told, not so much by the Governor of the Bank of England but by international speculators, that the policies on which we had fought the election could not be implemented; that the Government was to be forced into the adoption of Tory policies to which it was fundamentally opposed. The Governor confirmed that this was, in fact, the case.

I asked him if this meant that it was impossible for any Government, whatever its party label, whatever its manifesto or the policies on which it fought an election, to continue unless it immediately reverted to full-scale Tory policies. He had to admit that this was what his argument meant, because of the sheer compulsion of the economic dictation of those who exercised decisive economic power.[28]

But here's the rub. The tale of reformist governments defeated by economic constraints imposed notably through the flight of capital on the financial markets is almost as old as social democracy itself. Blair's is the first Labour government since MacDonald's short-lived 1924 administration not, as yet, to have faced a major financial crisis. Usually the effect of these crises is to leave the government fatally weakened. This was true even of the great reforming Attlee government after the crisis induced by the sterling's return to convertibility in August 1947; it was also true of MacDonald's second administration, destroyed by the 'bankers' ramp' of August 1931; of the Wilson government, undermined by the succession of panics culminating in the devaluation of November 1967; and of the Wilson–Callaghan government, caught between haemorrhaging capital and militant labour during the onset of the first great postwar slump in 1974–6.

This record at the very least puts into question the idea that globalization has introduced radically new economic constraints on government action. Even when financial markets were much more tightly regulated than they are today (exchange controls were only scrapped in Britain by the Thatcher government in 1979), Labour governments were forced to change course by international capital flight. Deregulation and the greater integration of financial markets over the past twenty years may have reinforced the structural limits on state action – what (according to Wilson) Cromer called 'the sheer compulsion of the economic dictation of those who exercised decisive economic power' – but they did not create them.

Of course, the past two decades have seen notable cases of social-democrat politicians humbled by markets. The most important of these episodes was the experience of the French

Socialist Party at the start of François Mitterrand's presidency, forced by a succession of currency crises between 1981 and 1983 to abandon its policies of Keynesian reflation and wholesale nationalization and to adopt instead a version of Thatcherism. The most recent case was the left-wing social democrat Oskar Lafontaine's eviction from the German Finance Ministry in March 1999, after a concerted campaign against his tax proposals by German big business. As the *Financial Times* put it, 'the leaders of German industry have claimed their scalp.' The paper rather gloatingly compared the affair with Mitterrand's: 'Mr Mitterrand's government had two years in power before executing its *volte face*. Mr Lafontaine concertinad that process into little more than four months before his politics met the combined resistance of the European Central Bank and German businesses threatening to switch to locations elsewhere.'[29]

Yet, set against the background of the history briefly recounted above, these episodes, undeniably important though they are, seem indicative less of the impact of globalization than of a more fundamental constraint on governments not to engage in actions that threaten the viability of capital, national as well as international. Lafontaine's fall was a victory for *German* capital – not anonymous multinational corporations or even the 'gnomes of Zurich' denounced by Harold Wilson a generation earlier, but of, for example, the twenty-two corporate leaders who lobbied the Chancellor, Gerhard Schröder, demanding that he discipline his Finance Minister. Much discussion of the political implications of economic globalization is vitiated by a failure to distinguish between the genuine consequences of greater economic integration and the more elemental requirements of capital reproduction *tout court*.

1.3 Myths of the 'New Economy'

The sense that we are living in a new social world nevertheless remains central to Third Way thinking. Thus Blair pronounces: 'I believe it is no exaggeration to say that we are in the middle of the greatest economic, technological and social upheaval that the world has seen since the industrial revolution began over two hundred years ago.'[30] *Living on Thin Air*, by Blair's adviser Charles Leadbeater, seeks to substantiate this vision. Written in a bright gee-whiz style, full of autobiographical asides and reverent pen portraits of dynamic 'knowledge entrepreneurs', the book is a latter-day version of Samuel Smiles' *Self Help*, a dithyramb sung to the glory of contemporary capitalism.[31]

Leadbeater is in fact ambivalent about whether his love-object can still be described as capitalism. 'We are moving into a post-capitalist society,' he announces. This society will be both 'open and innovative, and yet inclusive and co-operative'. The force driving us towards this utopia is the 'knowledge economy'. No longer do we survive by the physical production of material goods: 'We're all in the thin-air business these days ... the real assets of the modern economy come out of our heads not out of the ground: ideas, knowledge, skills, talent and creativity.'[32]

Successful companies today are those that are able to come up with a popular brand, and increasingly branding depends not on association with any particular product, but on tapping the resources of new knowledge generated by an increasingly science-based society. Best adapted to this task are not giant multinational corporations, but smaller, free-wheeling, more entrepreneurial firms with informal, non-bureaucratic structures that maximize creativity, linked together in decentralized networks. The new 'knowledge capitalism' thus brings with it not a further concentration of economic power but rather its greater dispersion. Thus, in classic Third Way mode, we can have our cake and eat it – combine the capitalist dynamism celebrated by the New Right with the social justice sought by the Old Left.

This argument depends on a series of elisions. Critically these involve the equation of creativity and entrepreneurship. Thus among Leadbeater's homilies are the stories of people who have been able to bring some real improvements to run-down working-class areas. These no doubt admirable persons are portrayed as 'social entrepreneurs' possessing essentially the same skills as are required to turn a profit in the business world. Private business is thereby given a caring gloss, while simultaneously a free-enterprise model is implicitly offered as the answer to poverty and inequality. Meanwhile, the very expression 'knowledge capitalism' suggests, as Leadbeater unrelentingly insists, that scientific innovation is the exclusive property of the private sector. The trouble is that, as he is sometimes forced to acknowledge, this is entirely false – the scientific research behind the technological change he breathlessly celebrates is largely a product of the public sector: 'This explosion of scientific knowledge was made possible by huge state investment in research, particularly through two world wars and the Cold War.'[33]

The Internet is a case in point – the creation of DARDA, the Pentagon's research agency. As Castells puts it, 'the state, not the innovative entrepreneur in his garage, both in America and throughout the world, was the initiator of the information technology revolution.'[34] Indeed, the kind of knowledge entrepreneurship Leadbeater so admires seems often to involve the looting of fundamental research performed at public expense to the benefit of greedy and ambitious private individuals. He concedes the point when, in a revealing metaphor, he declares: 'Universities should be the open-cast mines of the knowledge economy.'[35] The new 'post-capitalism' thus turns out to be more like a parasite, getting ideas by asset-stripping publicly funded research. No wonder that Leadbeater is unable to say anything coherent or interesting about one of the most serious threats to the entire process of scientific research – the go-ahead given by both the US government and the European Union to companies to patent genes. A capitalism so ravenous that it strives to consume not just the world itself but those abstract properties of nature revealed by scientific research hardly fits into his cosy picture of the future.

Leadbeater doesn't completely ignore the downside. He acknowledges that even his beloved Silicon Valley 'has a weak civic culture and ... is a highly unequal society'. Indeed, he goes so far as to concede that 'I am very well aware that the acute and chronic insecurity and inequality generated by this stage of globalization is the biggest issue for most people and that the measures proposed in this book to tackle rising inequality do not go far enough.' You can say that again. Leadbeater says 'we must innovate *and* include', but the general drift of his public policy proposals is further to reinforce the processes that have over the past two decades so widened social inequalities. He looks forward to the withering away of the modern tax system and a state of affairs in which individuals' access to social security is dependent on their investment choices. For the public sector generally, therefore, the future holds the prospect of yet more privatization. Schools, for example, should be taken over by 'new kinds of democratically accountable intermediaries ... associations created by schools, services run by charities and private companies', though Leadbeater doesn't bother to explain how charities or private companies could be held to account.[36]

His casual arguments reveal a stunning insensitivity to the real differences in individuals' access to resources and therefore in their life-chances. Consider, for example, the following passage: 'Most of us earn our livings providing service, judgement, information or analysis, whether in a telephone call-centre, a lawyer's office, a government department or a scientific laboratory.' Sure – in the advanced economies, most of us produce services. But we do so under radically different conditions. A call-centre operator, doing a low-paid, highly supervised, semi-automated job (Leadbeater himself describes call centres as the 'factories' of the 'modern service economy'), lives in another world from that of, say, the head of the research department of a Wall Street investment bank wondering whether her next bonus will be four or five million dollars.[37] Yet both are service workers. The category is of little use analytically because it does not register differences in what Marx called the relations of production – the huge disparity in the incomes of call-centre operator and investment banker reflect their different positions in the structure of economic power at work and on the labour market. Such considerations don't seem to interest Leadbeater. In a remarkably Smilesian passage he acknowledges that, 'for most people, just getting by in a more competitive culture has become increasingly demanding and uncertain. Success in the new economy requires inner resources of confidence and resilience that most of us lack.' He doesn't want to throw those unable to keep up on the scrap-heap – they should be treated compassionately, and provided with 'more supportive yet flexible institutions which will pick us up when we fall down'. But it is only fair that what F. E. Smith called the glittering prizes should go to those tough enough to stay in the race – people like Leadbeater himself, who, he tells us, having traded up from being a journalist to become an independent consultant, now lives on his wits (indeed he offers a rather naïve list of the – relatively paltry, it has to be said – material rewards that these wits have earned – foreign holidays, mobile phones, computers, microwaves, people-carriers . . .).[38]

Manuel Castells' analysis of what he calls the 'network society' is at an altogether different level of scientific seriousness from Leadbeater's light-minded reveries. Yet his work is akin to Leadbeater's in that it too argues that the late twentieth century saw a qualitative break in socio-economic development associated with what he calls the 'information technology revolution'. Moreover, this change (as the expression the 'network society' suggests) has involved a dispersion of economic power among decentralized networks. This does not, however, signify 'the demise of capitalism'. Indeed,

> for the first time in history, the capitalist mode of production shapes social relationships over the entire planet. But this brand of capitalism is profoundly different from its historical predecessors. It has two fundamental characteristics: it is global, and it is structured to a large extent around a network

of financial flows. Capital works globally as a unit in real time, and it is realized, invested, and accumulated mainly in the sphere of circulation, that is as finance capital.[39]

It is neither appropriate nor feasible for me to discuss here in any detail the arguments of a massive and complex work that ranges very widely and draws on Castells' own research. I wish instead to focus on three issues directly relevant to the broader debate on the Third Way. The first concerns how Castells conceptualizes what he calls 'informational capitalism', the second addresses the metaphor of the 'network society', while the third is directed at the claims he (along with many others) makes for the 'information technology revolution'.

To take the first question: Castells was originally a Marxist urban geographer, and continues to use a theoretical vocabulary that draws heavily on Marxist concepts (though often not terribly rigorously – thus in the passage cited above, it is hard to see how capital of any form can realize itself *except* in the sphere of circulation, that is, through the sale of commodities). He distinguishes accordingly between 'modes of production (capitalism, statism) and modes of development (industrialism, informationalism)'. A mode of production is presumably defined by the relations of production, that is, by the relations of effective control over the productive forces. In orthodox Marxist treatments the relations of production are normally contrasted with the productive forces, which comprise the material elements of production (labour-power and means of production) and the scientific knowledge and technical know-how required to operate them. But Castells introduces the notion of 'mode of development', which seems to operate as a kind of intermediary between the forces and relations of production:

> Modes of development are the technological arrangements through which labour works on matter to generate the product, ultimately determining the level and quality of surplus. Each mode of development is defined by the element that is fundamental to fostering productivity in the production process.[40]

In the case of 'informationalism' this element is 'the action of knowledge upon knowledge itself'. Moreover:

> Each mode of development has also a structurally determined performance principle around which technological processes are organized: industrialism is oriented towards economic growth, that is toward maximizing output; informationalism is oriented towards technological development, that is toward the accumulation of knowledge and towards higher levels of complexity in information processing.[41]

This account implies that, 'while informationalism is linked to the expansion and rejuvenation of capitalism', the resulting socio-economic transformation cannot be reduced to the logic of capital accumulation.[42] The technological mode of development apparently gives economic actors motivations independent of those that they derive from their place in capitalist relations of production. This seems dubious on both empirical and theoretical grounds. 'Industrialism', according to Castells, gave priority to maximizing growth. But, in fact, of course, companies often pursued (and indeed continue to pursue) strategies aimed at restricting output. Monopolies and cartels are particular forms of this kind of strategy. These strategies are pursued as a way of maintaining or increasing profitability. Capitalist relations of production involve a structure of competitive accumulation that gives individual capitals powerful incentives to maximize profitability, even if this means sacrificing growth.

Has this state of affairs changed under the 'informationalist mode of development'? Not obviously. The movement to 'higher levels of complexity in information processing' seems, more often than not, to be the consequence of profit-maximizing strategies. Thus every successive version of Microsoft's operating system requires more and more powerful computers to run it: the result is to leave existing computer-owners with the unpalatable choice between sticking with their old machine, risking cutting themselves off from the latest applications, or investing in a new model, which will itself soon become obsolescent. This constant pressure to upgrade is driven not by any autonomous technological imperative, but by the interest in profit-maximization shared by Microsoft, Intel and the PC manufacturers.

Robert Brenner has suggested that each set of production relations comprises 'rules of reproduction' that mandate the strategies economic actors must pursue if they are to maintain their position in these relations. In the case of capitalists these rules require them to make productivity-enhancing investments that will allow them to remain profitable and competitive. It is this process of competitive accumulation that is responsible for the dynamic development of the productive forces under capitalism.[43] Castells' account of the industrialist and informationalist 'modes of development' suggests that the 'performance principles' that these involve might override or operate independently of capitalist rules of reproduction. But this is not so. These rules may lead to profound technical transformations with enormous social consequences, but the reason why these changes are undertaken have to do not with abstract considerations related to increasing output or knowledge, but with the more mundane search for higher profits.[44]

At points Castells concedes as much, writing, for example: *'Profitability and competitiveness are the actual determinants of technological innovation and productivity growth.'*[45] But he does not consider the damaging implications of such statements for his conception of an autonomous technological mode of development. The resulting incoherence is illustrated by the fact that he claims as his inspiration *both* the theorists of post-industrialism, Daniel Bell and Alain Touraine *and* the Althusserian Marxist Nicos Poulantzas.[46] The concept of 'informational capitalism' is thus an unstable and eclectic compromise between what are in fact two rival research programmes – the Marxist theory of the capitalist mode of production and the theory of post-industrial society, one of whose main purposes is to show that the advanced societies at least have transcended the characteristic antagonisms of capitalist society.[47]

This argument is an important one: for Castells the 'net-

work society' arose from 'the interaction between these two
relatively autonomous trends: the development of new information technologies and the old society's attempt to retool
itself by using the power of technology to serve the technology of power'.[48] The implication is that 'informationalism' can escape its capitalist carapace.

There is, of course, an
obvious sense in which this is a perfectly orthodox Marxist
idea – one factor driving us towards socialism is supposed to
be the struggle of the new productive forces to break free of
their capitalist integument. But Castells seems to suggest sometimes (though in a much less crass way than Leadbeater)
that the new post-capitalist society is already here.

This is most evident in the second theme I wish to address
– the very idea of a network society itself. Informational
capitalism involves, Castells claims, a new 'organizational
logic', which is that of the network. '*Networks are the
fundamental stuff of which new organizations are and will
be made.*' The old corporation – hierarchically organized,
functionally differentiated, vertically integrated – is in crisis.
In its place comes 'the network enterprise: *that specific form
of enterprise whose system of means is constituted by the
intersection of segments of autonomous systems of goals*'.[49]
This is hardly a very perspicuous definition, but its essential
meaning is conveyed by the metaphor of the network itself –
power is dispersed among autonomous centres caught up in
a web of mutual dependence.

Castells is careful to proclaim not the death of the big
corporation, but rather its transformation, 'from *multinational enterprises* to *international networks*'. Thus 'multinational corporations are indeed the power-holders of wealth
and technology in the global economy, since most networks
are structured around such corporations. But at the same
time, they are internally differentiated in decentralized networks and externally dependent on their membership of a
complex changing structure of interlocking networks.' The
result is interdependence rather than domination: 'the networks are asymmetrical, but each single network can hardly
survive by its own or impose its diktat. The logic of the

network is more powerful than the powers in the network.'
Thus: 'Power still exists, but it is randomly exercised.'[50]
These remarks ma___ ___an no more than that in the contemporary _____ y individual capitals are caught up
i_ _____tion that none, even in the largest,
_____s is perfectly true, but is a constitu-
_____talist economy: it does not serve to
_____ork society' from its predecessors.
_____ulgar leftist (or in fascist) critiques do a
_____olists get together to pull the strings.
_____ necessarily involved in a structure of
_____dence that they cannot individually or
_____inate.
_____, of course, that nothing has changed.
_____as seen a massive process of capitalist
_____ionally organized capitalisms that pre-
_____ng, between the First World War and
_____n cracked open and drawn into a far
_____lobal economy. As international compe-
t_____ified, corporations have been transformed
th_____sizing, de-layering, and the like. As we saw
in _____e, multinationals do often rely on the develop-
me__ __omplex supply networks. Moreover, as Castells
stre_____, the IT revolution has made possible the development of new forms of managerial control. But to describe
this process in the terms that he does when he writes that
'the globalization of competition dissolves the large corpor-
ation in a web of multidirectional networks' is to descend
into vulgar apologetics.[51]

Apart from anything else, this ignores the vast mergers and
acquisitions boom that helped to drive the US and European
stock markets during the past decade or so. Mergers and
acquisitions have grown at an annual rate of 42 per cent over
the past two decades, with a completed value in 1999 of
$2,300 billion, equivalent to 8 per cent of world gross dom-
estic product.[52] Far from 'dissolving', multinational corporations have been involved in a desperate Darwinian struggle to
expand or die. Any reader of the business press will be

familiar with the regular reports predicting greater concentration in this or that sector. Over-capacity in the world car industry has produced particularly powerful pressure on firms to team up through take-overs and alliances. But this process is very far from being an 'Old Economy' phenomenon. In telecommunications, entertainment and IT itself the same forces are at work. Castells himself notes the 'increasingly oligopolistic' tendencies in the global media industry, whose most spectacular result so far has been the $127 billion take-over of the vast Time Warner entertainment and media empire by America Online in January 2000.[53]

Richard Tomkins has recently claimed that the tendencies towards concentration and centralization are even greater among Internet companies. Despite the fact that there are far fewer barriers to entry to the Internet than in more traditional sectors, 'as the business-to-consumer market develops, there are signs that it is becoming an online version of the winner-take-all society: one in which two or three companies at the top take a vastly disproportionate share of the market, making it difficult for others to thrive.' Tomkins argues that globalization, in combination with technical improvements in communication, has allowed big companies to realize enormous economies of scale by treating large regions or even the world as a single market. These economies are even greater on the Internet, since the cost of distributing output to a wider customer base is zero. At the same time the value of Internet services to advertisers increases the more people use them, favouring well-established firms such as Amazon and Yahoo over newcomers: by late 2000, 71 per cent of US dotcom advertising was going to the top ten sites. One investment analyst 'foresees the survival of only three or four dotcom companies in the business-to-consumer world'.[54]

The even bigger corporations that are emerging from the mergers and acquisition frenzy indeed possess highly differentiated structures. Large private enterprises are liable to the same kind of bureaucracy-induced irrationality (so-called X-inefficiency) as the old Stalinist command economies, and various managerial strategies are deployed to address this problem. But to treat this complex process of economic centralization as having merely 'random' implications for the distribution of power seems simply frivolous. Within MNCs, to the extent that major investment decisions are made in the company headquarters, power remains 'asymmetrically' distributed. When BMW decided to get rid of its Rover subsidiary in March 2000, the Blair government discovered it was Munich that called the shots, not the local management in Birmingham and Oxford (let alone the politicians at Westminster). On the larger political scene, the sheer size and wealth of the big corporations gives them enormous influence, particularly where, as in the US and Britain, the major parties are largely dependent on business donations to finance their electoral campaigns.

A regrettable descent into boosterism is also evident in the third of Castells' themes that I wish to discuss, namely the claims he makes for the IT revolution itself. It is, he says, 'as major an historical event as was the eighteenth-century industrial revolution, inducing a pattern of discontinuity in the material basis of economy, society, and culture'. Such claims are, of course, familiar enough in the general euphoric hubbub surrounding the 'New Economy' in the US. Like other contributors to this genre Castells relies heavily on extrapolations from the admittedly spectacular growth rates of the 1990s, which leave him confident enough to declare: 'By the turn of the century, the Internet economy and, the information technology industries had become the core of the economy – not only qualitatively but quantitatively.'[55]

Such claims are difficult to separate from the more general argument about whether or not, as Alan Greenspan famously put it, the US economy has gone 'beyond history' – that is, whether the long boom of the 1990s and, in particular, the higher rates of productivity growth recorded since the middle of the decade reflect the impact of the IT revolution, which has put the economy on a long-term low-inflation, high-growth path. For Greenspan, '[a] perceptible quickening in the pace at which technological innovations

are applied argues for the hypothesis that the recent acceler-
ation in labour productivity is not just a cyclical phenomenon or a statistical aberration, but reflects, at least in part,
a more deep-seated, still developing shift in our economic
landscape.'[56] Castells himself enters the controversy over
whether or not there has been a reversal of the long stagnation of US productivity growth since the early 1970s, citing
the boom itself in evidence: 'In fact, only a substantial
productivity increase could explain the economic boom in
the US in 1994–9.'[57]

Precisely the opposite case is argued from within an
impeccably orthodox neo-classical framework by the economist Robert J. Gordon. He contends, on the basis of careful
econometric analysis, that the fact that the annual rate of
growth of US labour productivity rose in 1995–9 to 2.15
per cent – well above the dismal 1.13 per cent average of
1972–95 but still significantly below the 2.63 per cent
average of 1950–72 – is to be explained as the product of
three factors: (1) changes in the measurement of national
income; (2) the characteristic feature of business cycles that,
when output increases more rapidly than the trend rate, the
number of hours worked tends also to grow, but not as fast:
consequently output per hour (labour productivity) rises; (3)
a genuine explosion of productivity – an annual rate of
growth of ouput per hour in 1995–9 of 41.7 per cent – but
one confined to the sector manufacturing computers, representing 1.2 per cent of the US non-farm private economy:
Gordon estimates that in the non-farm, non-durable sector –
87 per cent of the economy – productivity growth actually
fell during this period.[58]

Gordon's paper raises highly complex and controversial
issues in an area where a non-expert would be wise to tread
warily. But his carefully framed analysis does at least suggest
that the claims made for the 'New Economy' need to be
taken with a large pinch of salt. It also implies that the
impact of information technology has been much more
narrowly focused than might be suggested by analogies such
as those drawn by both Blair and Castells with the Industrial

Revolution at the turn of the eighteenth century. In another paper, Gordon develops a systematic comparison between the IT revolution and what is often called the Second Industrial Revolution in the late nineteenth and early twentieth centuries. This involved five 'clusters' of 'Great Inventions' – electric light and motors; the internal combustion engine and its spin-offs, including air travel, suburbanization, motorways and supermarkets; petroleum, natural gas, chemicals, plastics and pharmaceuticals; the transformation of entertainment and communication thanks to the telegraph, gramophone, popular photography, radio, cinema and television; running water, indoor plumbing and urban sanitation infrastructure. Gordon argues that the combined impact of these innovations transformed everyday life much more dramatically than the changes currently underway in the late twentieth and early twenty-first centuries, and underlay the 'golden years' of productivity growth between 1913 and 1970 at far higher rates than in either earlier or later periods.

The IT revolution is, he suggests, a much more narrowly based phenomenon: the nominal demand for computers has grown steadily since their invention at the start of the 1950s, but this reflects the spectacular but consistent fall in the price of computer power. The marginal utility of greater computer power is diminishing commensurately: the principal economic benefit of word-processing (eliminating repetitive typing and facilitating editing) came during the initial diffusion of micro-computers, and is little enhanced by new software packages. Meanwhile, computers continue to make up a relatively small proportion of capital stock. The Internet has made no perceptible impact on this state of affairs. While it may provide easier and cheaper access to information and entertainment, it involves shifting existing activities from one medium to another – logging on instead of going to the library – rather than freeing time in the way in which, say, the invention of the washing machine eliminated the terrible physical burden of hand-washing. Gordon is also sceptical about the impact of the Internet on productivity, suggesting that it allows employees to engage in their own pursuits –

day-trading on the stock market or ordering books from Amazon – on their employers' time.[59]

Gordon's arguments are a welcome corrective to the hype about the e-economy. Looking at the IT revolution from the perspective of *la longue durée* is a salutary experience. Those, for example, who might argue that the development of the Internet has had a bigger impact on everyday life than the introduction of indoor plumbing would only confirm the widespread suspicions about the personal hygiene of computer nerds. Even in the case of more recent technological changes, it is not obvious that the IT revolution has had the largest impact on how we live. Consider, for example, the effects of the development a generation ago, well before the IT 'revolution' took off, of cheap long-distance air travel in facilitating mass tourism, promoting trans-continental migration, and allowing families divided by once impossible distances to maintain regular face-to-face contact. Hasn't the Jumbo jet changed our lives more than the fact that we can now book our flights on-line?

These considerations leave open the question of the actual causes of the American boom. If an IT-based 'New Economy' wasn't responsible, what was? The work of Brenner and other Marxist economists has shown that the US, along with the other major Western economies, has faced a chronic crisis of profitability since the late 1960s. The brutal restructuring of the US economy over the past two decades has effected a partial recovery in profitability, thanks especially to the unprecedented decline in real hourly earnings for a quarter of a century.[60]

It is against this background that Wall Street has boomed, pushing share prices to levels way out of line with underlying company earnings. The Wall Street bubble has been a crucial component of the prolonged boom since the early 1990s: thanks to the so-called 'wealth effect', middle-class Americans have reacted to the increase in the value of their stock-market investments by borrowing and spending more. This allowed the US to act as 'consumer of last resort', helping to restabilize the world economy after the Asian and Russian crashes in 1997–8. But as Bill Martin and Wynne Godley have shown in a series of papers for the fund managers Phillips & Drew, the result is a formidable set of financial imbalances. The consumer boom is reflected not merely in a growing balance of payments deficit, but in private-sector indebtedness rising to unprecedented levels. Maintaining consumer spending in these circumstances would require share prices to continue rising at unsustainable rates. When – not if – the market begins seriously to fall, the 'wealth effect' will go into reverse: Martin and Godley predict that, as middle-class households respond to falling share-prices by cutting back on spending, the impact on the US and the world economies is likely to be severe.[61]

Martin's and Godley's work shows that you don't have to be a Marxist to think that the New Economy will go belly up. Two of the most persistent critics of the boosterism surrounding the Wall Street bubble are the *Financial Times'* leading economic commentators, Samuel Brittan and Martin Wolf, both of them firmly committed to neo-liberal orthodoxy. Brittan, who could with justification claim to have invented Thatcherite economics before Thatcher herself, dismisses assertions about 'Wall Street's ability to reach the stratosphere' as 'nonsense on stilts'. He adds, however, 'no one can say whether the break will come within one week, one year, or five years.'[62]

It is indeed the fact that the Wall Street bubble has yet to burst that has helped to sustain the hype surrounding the 'New Economy'. Financial markets are notoriously driven by irrational surges of fear and greed. One effect of the Asian and Russian crashes was to attract capital to the US as a haven of stability, thereby helping to keep the boom going, which has drawn yet more capital there (this is perhaps the main factor behind the euro's 25 per cent fall against the dollar after its launch at the beginning of 1999). But the arguments and evidence adduced by the critics suggest that this virtuous cycle cannot go on for ever. When it comes to an end, the boosters will look as foolish as their counterparts did after the Wall Street crash of October 1929.

2

Guardians of Morals

2.1 Back to values

In April 1999 various centre-left leaders met in Washington to discuss the Third Way. The event – very much a feel-good affair pervaded by mutual congratulations occasioned in particular by the role of those present in initiating and sustaining the NATO bombardment of Yugoslavia – was the occasion of the following incident (I use here Slavoj Žižek's version of a widely retailed anecdote): 'the Italian Prime Minister Massimo d'Alema said that one should not be afraid of the word "socialism". Clinton and, following him, Blair and Schröder, are supposed to have burst out laughing.'[1]

In fact, according to the official record, d'Alema, over-come perhaps by his journey from the Communist Party Youth to the White House, managed to make this remark without actually uttering the S-word.[2] Little wonder, then, that later that same year Blair tried unsuccessfully to per-suade the Second International to change its name to the Centre-Left International, and thereby to allow the Clinton–Gore Democratic Party to join.

In fact, however, despite this distaste for the word 'social-ism', the concept is not entirely absent from Third Way thinking, at least on this side of the Atlantic. It survives in the shape of the timeless values that, as we have seen, the centre-left seeks to adapt to contemporary conditions. Thus Blair told the Washington seminar the Third Way is 'about reasserting ourselves as a party of values', 'a rediscovery of our essential values – the belief in community, opportunity and responsibility'.[3]

Indeed an emphasis on values – in particular that of community – has been a persistent feature of Blair's leader-ship of the Labour Party. Early on he sought to appropriate a traditional conservative concern with social cohesion, adopting the slogan even before he became party leader 'tough on crime, tough on the causes of crime', and denoun-cing Thatcherism for its promotion of atomistic individual-ism: 'In fact, duty is an essential Labour concept. It is at the heart of creating a strong community or society. It is the only way of making sense of the rules by which people wish to lead their lives in a modern age. Without it, we are left either with a crude form of individualism, or an overbearing state.'[4] This stress on duty was embodied in what has become the New Labour mantra that 'rights and responsibil-ities go together'.

More recently, at a low point in his premiership during the summer of 2000, Blair delivered a lecture under the auspices of the dissident Catholic theologian Hans Küng at Tübingen University. It was chiefly noticed at the time for the silly, and almost immediately abandoned, proposal to allow the police to impose on-the-spot fines for antisocial behaviour. But the lecture was also notable for a particularly strong affirmation of community as the master-virtue. Seek-ing to define 'traditional values', Blair declared:

For me, they are best expressed in a modern idea of com-munity. At the heart of it is the belief in the equal worth of all [–] the central belief that drives my politics – and in our mutual responsibility in creating a society that advances such equal worth. Note: it is equal worth, not equality of income or outcome; or simply, equality of opportunity. Rather, it affirms our equal right to dignity, liberty, freedom from discrimination as well as economic opportunity. The idea of community resolves the paradox of the modern world: it acknowledges our interdependence; it recognizes our individual worth.[5]

If socialism survives in Third Way ideology it does so as an ethical socialism that gives priority to community. Indeed, in the early 1990s Blair was willing to use the S-word, but hyphenated as 'social-ism', to stress the weight he gave to community in his version of the concept. There seem in fact to be three main strands in Third Way ethics: first, community, the all-subsuming concept; secondly, equality; and thirdly, the extension of the idea of community to the international domain in the shape of 'ethical' foreign policy and the doctrine of humanitarian intervention. I consider this third strand in the next chapter; the other two represent the subject matter of the present chapter.

2.2   Egalitarianism betrayed

Given the priority Blair accords community, it may seem counter-intuitive to start with equality. But Norberto Bobbio has argued that, despite the collapse of 'existing socialism', 'there is a very clear distinction between the right and the left, for which equality has always been the pole star that guides it.'[6] The growth of social inequality both within countries and on a global scale over the past two decades has indeed made the issue a highly urgent one, as Bobbio stresses. The theoretical and practical stance taken up on this issue by advocates of the Third Way is therefore a litmus test of their claim to be renewing the left. Moreover, the fact that the New Labour government in Britain has sought to pursue a serious strategy for reducing inequality devised by the Chancellor of the Exchequer, Gordon Brown, allows us to bring the issue into focus.[7] Brown, who exerts a dominance in New Labour domestic policy unusual in finance ministers (despite Blair's flaunted presidentialism, his government is in many respects a dyarchy), has been ready to give the issue of equality a high profile. Thus, when the government was in the doldrums in the summer of 2000, Brown took advantage of a row over Oxford's admissions procedures to denounce old school tie elitism and affirm New Labour's commitment to 'opportunity for all'. His strategy has in fact four main components.

(1) The equality sought is equality of opportunity. Third Way ideologues regularly denounce 'equality of outcome', which they associate with the Old Left. Giddens, for example, argues that 'the "egalitarianism at all costs" that absorbed leftists for so long' is obsolete, advocating instead 'a dynamic model of egalitarianism'.[8] Equality of outcome is pretty much a red herring, since it is hard to come up with anyone, at least in contemporary debates, who has advocated placing everyone in precisely the same material situation.

Thus one of the main themes in the extraordinarily rich and sophisticated discussions of equality that have developed among political philosophers such as Ronald Dworkin, Amartya Sen and G. A. Cohen in response to John Rawls' *A Theory of Justice* has been that egalitarians should seek to remedy the harmful consequences of 'brute luck' – of accidents outside individuals' control such as the natural talents or the class position that they have inherited. Once, however, access to advantage has thus been equalized, individuals are responsible for whatever use they make of the resources that have been allocated to them. The inevitably different outcomes that then emerge will not be unjust, since the effects of brute luck – from whose consequences no one deserves to suffer – have been eliminated.[9]

(2) A charitable reading of Brown's conception of 'opportunities for all' would treat it as in fact a version of this kind

of egalitarianism. More concretely, it is a case of what Stuart White calls '*endowment egalitarianism*', that is, equalizing 'the background distribution of productive endowments so that market interactions lead to a greater initial equality of income, lessening the need for subsequent redistribution'.[10] In this case, however, it is access to only one productive endowment that is to be made more equal – namely skills, through improved education and training. This reflects Brown's more general belief that paid employment is the 'route to opportunity' – a belief informing, among other measures, his New Deal welfare-to-work programme for the long-term unemployed.

(3) This strategy is in any case economically desirable, since in the 'knowledge economy' competitiveness depends on the skills of the workforce. As Brown puts it, 'equality of opportunity is also an economic necessity. Economies that do not bring out the best in people will ossify and fall behind.'[11] This strategy thus rewards virtue – social justice doesn't conflict with, but enhances, economic efficiency. So Blair could reassure the Washington seminar that 'enterprise and justice can live together'.[12] Or, as Brown elaborated while still in Opposition: 'where the success and failure of an economy depend on access to knowledge more than access to capital, individual liberation arises from the enhancement of the value of labour rather than the abolition of private capital.'[13]

(4) In the background of Brown's pursuit of equality of opportunity lies his acceptance of neo-liberal economics in the relatively crude version known as monetarism that was developed by Milton Friedman and used to provide the rationale for the policies of the Thatcher government in the 1980s. In his 1999 Mais lecture Brown explicitly endorsed Friedman's revival of the classical liberal doctrine of the natural rate of unemployment.[14] This is the idea that the economy tends to an equilibrium rate of unemployment at which the rate of inflation is stable (the so-called 'Non-

Accelerating Inflation Rate of Unemployment', NAIRU).
According to Friedman and his followers, any attempt to
reduce the rate of unemployment below this level – through,
for example, Keynesian demand-management policies – will
simply cause the rate of inflation to rise without any long-
term increase in the rate of output or the level of
employment.[15]

In a more recent lecture Brown sought to associate his
economic policy with Maynard Keynes, Friedman's main
intellectual target. So he claims that 'it is this Government
that, in rejecting the short-termism – not least the crude
"Keynesianism" of past economic approaches – is seeking to
draw on the best of Keynes' insights about political economy
and put a modern Keynesian approach into practice.'[16] Like
any interesting thinker, Keynes is often open to more than
one interpretation, and can therefore be claimed, with vary-
ing degrees of plausibility, by different intellectual traditions.
But it is hard to see how the thought of an economist who
could write that 'in a world ruled by uncertainty with an
uncertain future linked to an actual present, a final state of
equilibrium, such as one deals with in static economies, does
not properly exist' can easily be accommodated within the
kind of orthodox neo-classical equilibrium framework on
which the concept of the NAIRU depends.[17]

In fact Brown's main intellectual reference point in both
these texts seems rather to be an earlier Mais lecture, delivered in 1984, by Nigel Lawson, Tory Chancellor of the
Exchequer 1983–9, and the dominant figure in economic
policy-making under Thatcher. Thus he praises Lawson for
arguing that '[i]t is the conquest of inflation, and not the
pursuit of growth and employment, which is or should be
the objective of macro-economic policy. And it is the creation of conditions conducive to growth and employment,
and not the suppression of price rises, which is or should be
the objective of micro-economic policy.'[18]

It is true that Brown criticizes Lawson for engineering an
inflationary boom in the late 1980s that led, predictably
enough, to recession at the start of the 1990s. Yet Lawson's

two main objectives, as spelled out in the passage just quoted, were essentially the same as Brown's. In the first place, Lawson, like Brown, believed that the main macro-economic role of government is to achieve a low rate of inflation through fiscal and monetary stability. He sought various proxies that could, he hoped, play the kind of role the Gold Standard had undertaken before 1914 by keeping the economy on autopilot, outside the control of elected politicians. After the failure of successive monetary targets – first a series of measures of the money supply and then the sterling–Deutschmark exchange rate – to perform this function, Lawson came to the conclusion, by the time he resigned as Chancellor in October 1989, that control over monetary policy should be transferred to the Bank of England. This measure was, of course, Brown's first act in government after the May 1997 general election.[19]

Secondly, Lawson sought to reduce the natural rate of unemployment or NAIRU. According to monetarist doctrine, this can only be done by micro-economic measures designed to increase the profitability of hiring labour. Reducing long-term unemployment is thus a matter of changing the supply side of the labour market. Brown's main difference here with Lawson is that his emphasis is less on reducing wages and weakening unions than on increasing productivity via improved education and training. Thus he calls for 'an active supply side policy . . . not only to sustain low inflation but to improve productivity and employment. . . . And to achieve that productivity, we need more than deregulation: we need radical labour[,] capital and product market reforms.'[20] We thus see that, paradoxically, Brown's formula for reconciling economic efficiency and social equality depends upon his acceptance of the version of neo-liberal economics under whose hegemony British society became far more polarized between rich and poor than it had been for half a century.

There is a great deal that could be said about all this, and I have said some of it elsewhere.[21] Here I shall make just four main points. First of all, the idea that getting as many people as possible into paid employment is the key to reducing inequality is misconceived. This is partly because most members of some of the most disadvantaged groups – for example, the disabled and the elderly – cannot work. It is also because much depends on the nature and remuneration of the jobs on offer. The point has effectively been conceded recently by Margaret Hodge, the New Labour minister responsible for the welfare-to-work New Deal:

> Simply getting people into jobs is not enough. There is growing evidence from the States that poor and unqualified people who move into low-paid jobs will not move out of poverty, but are likely to move back into unemployment.
>
> This is confirmed by a recent British study of lone parents which found that among those lone parents who moved into work, a quarter stopped work again within a year, and half drifted in and out of unemployment for five years.[22]

Secondly, these considerations might seem to reinforce Brown's emphasis on helping to improve individuals' market capacity through improved education and training. But even some Third Way theorists are dubious about making education a panacea. Giddens observes: 'A great deal of comparative research, in the US and Europe, demonstrates that education tends to reflect wider economic inequalities and these have to be tackled at source.'[23] Indeed, according to Brown's own Treasury,

- if one father's earnings are double the level of another, his son's maths test score is on average five percentile points higher than the others and 2.7 percentile points up the reading test distribution.
- for a daughter the gain is five percentile points up the distribution of both maths and reading tests scores.[24]

Brown's intervention in the row over Oxford admissions procedures illustrated the Blair government's failure to address the way in which access to education reflects the more fundamental realities of class. Let us skirt over his absurd attempt to hold up to British universities as the very model of egalitarian entrance policies none other than Harvard, more accurately described by Godfrey Hodgson as 'proudly and unapologetically, both elite and elitist . . . ferociously competitive . . . also authoritarian and hierarchical'.[25]

Brown quite rightly attacked the gross inequity of an education system in which only 17 per cent of young people from lower socio-economic groups enter higher education, compared to 45 per cent of non-manual groups, and children from private schools account for 39 per cent of the entry to the top thirteen universities.[26] But, however opaque Oxbridge admissions procedures may be, they are unlikely to be the main cause of this state of affairs. A more obvious cause is the far greater resources devoted to each child attending what in Britain are laughingly called the public schools than to those in state schools. But New Labour is about as likely to scrap the tax subsidies public schools enjoy thanks to their charitable status as it is to nationalize the commanding heights of industry. Brown talks a good fight, but he has left untouched what R. H. Tawney called the 'barbarity' that 'differences of educational opportunity among children should depend upon differences of wealth among parents'.[27]

Thirdly, inequality has widened under New Labour. The Gini coefficient measuring inequality in income distribution rose from 33 in 1996–7 to 35 in 1998–9, the highest level since the Thatcher era.[28] According to the Department of Social Security, the number of people living in households on less than half the average income (the official definition of poverty) rose during the Blair government's first two years in office from 16.9 to 17.7 per cent of the population. The richest 10 per cent of the population saw their income rise by 7.1 per cent, compared to only 1.9 per cent for that of the poorest 10 per cent. While the number of children in poverty rose slightly, 80 per cent of the increase in the number of poor people came from a rise in the number of pensioners living below the poverty line from 2 to 2.4

million.[29] A study commissioned by the Joseph Rowntree Foundation and using a different definition of poverty found that 14.5 million people – 26 per cent of the UK population – were living in poverty by the end of 1999.[30]

The growth in poverty under New Labour is all the more striking since it took place at a time when the economy was growing relatively quickly. It is directly related to Brown's policies, and, in particular, his failure to reverse the Thatcher government's decision to tie increases in the state pension to the rate of inflation rather than the rate at which earnings rise. This led to a derisory 75 pence a week increase in the state pension in April 2000. Brown claimed to be addressing the plight of the poorest pensioners by providing them with a means-tested Minimum Income Guarantee. But the take-up of means-tested benefits is notoriously lower than when benefits are provided universally.

The traditional social-democratic strategy for reducing poverty has been the provision of universal benefits financed by redistributive taxation. Such an option is ruled out by New Labour's commitment to the neo-liberal policy intro-duced in the Thatcher government's first budget of shifting the fiscal burden from direct to indirect taxation (a policy that the IMF and World Bank are now pressing governments to apply generally). Brown boasts of having reduced corpor-ation tax to 30 per cent, the lowest level of business taxation in the major industrial countries.[31] The effect is to deprive governments of the main redistributive mechanism that could alleviate poverty by transferring resources from rich to poor. This does not mean that Brown has made no such use of fiscal policy: soon after taking office he mounted what John Plender calls 'one of the greatest raids on corporate cashflow in history' to finance the welfare-to-work New Deal.[32] Yet such ploys have not, as we have seen, prevented inequality from rising under New Labour. Meanwhile, the increasing burden of regressive indirect taxation helped to provoke the revolt against fuel prices in the autumn of 2000.

More generally Brown's insistence on demonstrating his 'prudence' by attempting to pursue more effectively the hard-

money policy of his predecessors crippled Blair's first administration. Even a journalist as close to the Blair court as the
Financial Times' Philip Stephens was prompted to protest:

> With the benefit of hindsight, it seems clear that it [New
> Labour] made a big political mistake in sticking to the
> Conservatives' spending targets for the first two years of the
> 1997 election.
>   Messrs Blair and Brown were fighting the last war rather
> than the next. A pledge that seemed eminently sensible while
> Labour languished in opposition was too tight a straightjacket
> [*sic*] for a party that had won such a crushing electoral
> victory. Expectations of a transformation in the condition of
> public services were allowed to run far ahead of reality. Much
> of the increased spending over the next few years will simply
> be repairing the damage of that early, self-imposed austerity.[33]

The brutal squeeze on public spending brought the long-
running crisis of the National Health Service, starved of
resources by successive governments since the 1970s, sharply
into focus. The substantial absolute rises in public spending
finally announced by Brown in his July 2000 spending
review would not begin to reverse the consequences of this
earlier clamp-down. Samuel Brittan pointed out that the
share of total managed expenditure in gross domestic product fell from 41.2 per cent in 1996–7, the last Tory year of
office, to 37.7 per cent in 1999–2000:

> Even in the terminal year of the new spending review,
> 2003–4, it is expected to reach only 40.5 per cent. It will not
> only be lower than in the last Conservative year but will be
> even further below the total reached in the early years of John
> Major's government [at the beginning of the 1990s], when it
> peaked at 44.1 per cent.[34]

Fourthly, the general upshot of these considerations is
that, hardly surprisingly, egalitarian aspirations cannot be
effectively grafted onto neo-liberal economics. The monetarist policies that have helped widen social and economic

inequalities especially in Britain and the United States have proved unable to harmonize 'enterprise and justice'. Third Way politicians in these countries have enjoyed a comparatively easy ride thanks to the American boom and its overspill in Britain. A recession that, as happened in Britain during the early 1990s, forced unemployment back up again and transformed massive budget surpluses into deficits would leave them facing an altogether less palatable set of choices.

Yet Brown's regular claims to have freed the British economy from 'boom and bust' suggest that he has fallen for the particularly naïve version of monetarist economics according to which the right mix of policies can allow capitalism to transcend the business cycle. In thus refusing to recognize the constitutive instability of capitalist economies – a theme, whatever the other differences between them, common to the thought too of Marx and Keynes, Schumpeter and Hayek – Gordon Brown has exceeded the ambitions even of his antagonistic twin Nigel Lawson. History is likely to have some surprises for him up its sleeve.

2.3 Community imposed

Community, like most interesting normative ideas, is a good example of what W. B. Gallie called essentially contested concepts, that is, 'concepts the proper use of which inevitably involves endless dispute about their proper uses'.[35] Gallie suggests that one source of these disputes is the internal complexity of such concepts: it is thus possible to come up with apparently valid but incompatible interpretations of the concept each of which lays emphasis on different aspects of its internally complex character. But another source of dispute arises from the larger discursive context of the concept under discussion. Concepts figure in discourse not on their own, but in combination, and the nature of this combination is likely to colour the reading of the individual concepts. Thus Alan Carling suggests that both socialists and supporters of the Third Way share the same core values – autonomy, community, democracy and equality.[36] This would seem to suggest a distinctly anti-authoritarian reading of the concept of community.

Things have, however, turned out differently, at least in the case of the Third Way. Thus numerous commentators have referred to the moral authoritarianism of the New Labour government. Jack Straw as Home Secretary in particular distinguished himself by his espousal of zero tolerance policing, attempts to restrict trial by jury, and persecution of asylum seekers. But Straw's record is symptomatic of the overall approach of the government, as a highly revealing leaked memo by Blair indicates. Writing at the end of April 2000, Blair largely accepted an agenda set by the authoritarian populism of the Tory right:

> There is a clutch of issues – seemingly disparate – that are in fact linked. We need a strategy that is almost discrete, focused on them. They are roughly combining 'on your side' issues with toughness and standing up for Britain. They range from: the family – where, partly due to MCA [i.e. the repeal of married couples' income tax allowance] and to gay issues, we are perceived as weak; asylum and crime where we are perceived as soft; and asserting the nation's interests where, because of the unpopularity of Europe, a constant barrage of small stories beginning to add up on defence and even issues like Zimbabwe, we are seen as insufficiently assertive.
>
> All this, of course, is perception. It is bizarre that any government I lead should be seen as anti-family. We are, in fact, taking very tough measures on asylum and crime. Kosovo should have laid to rest any doubts about our strength in defence. But all these things add up to a sense that the government – and this even applies to me – are somehow out of touch with gut British instincts.[37]

Blair's solution was to demand yet more toughness, for example against street crime in London:

> The Met police are putting in place more measures to deal with it; but as ever we lack a tough public message along

with the strategy. We should think now of an initiative, e.g. locking up street muggers. Something tough, with immediate bite, which sends a message through the system. . . . But this should be done soon, and I, personally, should be associated with it.

There is more to this than just the anxiety of a rather vain politician worried about his ratings in the opinion polls at a time when the Conservative Opposition had launched a vicious racist campaign against asylum seekers. When he himself was still Leader of the Opposition, Blair had already argued that the concept of duty should be given priority over that of rights:

Duty is the cornerstone of a decent society. It recognizes more than self. It defines the context in which rights are given. It is personal; but it is also owed to society. Respect for others, responsibility to them, is an essential prerequisite of a strong and active community. It is the method through which we can build a society that does not subsume our individuality but allows it to develop healthily. . . . The rights we receive should reflect the duties we owe. With the power should come the responsibility.[38]

Other exponents of the Third Way also downplay individual rights. Thus Giddens asks:

When the lives of local families are made miserable by racist groups of youths, would a street curfew after a certain hour add to the sum of available liberties or not? Should we try experimenting, as some have suggested, with urban safety zones in inner-city areas, where surveillance and saturation policing might create public spaces in which people could associate with each other? How far could and should electronic tagging replace conventional imprisonment or probation? However these questions are answered, the idea of substantive liberty is what matters – how far regulating some sorts of freedoms produces a net increase in freedom for communities as a whole.[39]

This passage – which is the only remark of any significant content that Giddens makes on the subject of rights in his two books on the Third Way – is, when one thinks about it, an astonishing thing for a leading mainstream Western intellectual to write at the beginning of the twenty-first century. In an important essay Ronald Dworkin argues that rights should be seen as 'trumps over some background justification for political decisions that states a goal for the community as a whole'. The most obvious example of such a background justification is what he calls unrestricted utilitarianism, which holds that the good consists in maximizing the general welfare even where this may seriously disadvantage individual members of society. Dworkin writes:

> We need rights as a distinct element in political theory, only when some decision that injures some people nevertheless finds *prima facie* support in the claim that it will make the community as a whole better off on some plausible account of where the community's general welfare lies. But the most natural source of any objection we might have to such a decision is that, in its concern with the welfare or prosperity or flourishing of people on the whole, or in the fulfilment of some interest, widespread within the community, the decision pays insufficient attention to its impact on the minority; and some appeal to equality seems a natural expression of an objection from that source. We want to say that the decision is wrong, in spite of its apparent merit, because it does not take the damage it causes to some into account in the right way and therefore does not treat these people as equals entitled to the same concern as others.[40]

This conception of rights as protection against the violation of the interests of minorities is, of course, a central theme of classical liberal thought. It is present in John Stuart Mill's *On Liberty*; it is expressed, in a somewhat different way from Dworkin, by John Rawls when he argues for the priority of liberty over equality in his two principles of justice. Yet Giddens breezily sweeps all these considerations aside – indeed, completely ignores them – as he asserts that liberty is something that can be maximized, so that it's OK to override individual liberties so long as 'the sum of available liberties' is increased. This is about as serious an argument as the justification that is often given (for example, by Jack Straw) for reducing the rights of suspects that this will protect the rights of the victims of crime – rights that often seem to come down to that of victims or their families to see convicted whoever the police claim is guilty of the crime in question irrespective of the actual evidence against them.[41]

I invoke the classical liberal argument in favour of rights with some embarrassment. Things have come to a pretty pass when a Marxist has to remind defenders of contemporary Western liberal societies of the point of the concepts constitutive of liberalism itself. But, as Theodor Adorno once put it, '[p]hilosophy, which once seemed obsolete, lives on because the moment to realize it was missed.'[42] The critics of liberal capitalism are entitled to demand that it lives up to its promise of guaranteeing individual liberty. To do so is not to treat rights as somehow absolute, or to dissolve society into the atomistic welter of warring individuals to which communitarian critics of liberalism claim the latter is committed. It is, rather, to demand that serious arguments are offered in favour of giving priority to duty over rights.

One might think of *The Principle of Duty*, by David Selbourne, as answering this demand. Selbourne is the guru of a neo-conservative camarilla of disillusioned ex-leftists and ex-feminists whose broodings have had some resonance in New Labour circles. He certainly *asserts* the priority of duty over rights, declaring that 'the performance of duty (to self, fellows, and the civic order) is the morally superior, as well as the historically prior, constituent of human association, especially when it is set against the claims of right.' And, rather like Blair, he proclaims 'a new *social-ism* founded upon an engagement to such duty' that will counter the disintegrative effects of liberal rights-based moralities.[43]

But there is nothing resembling an argument in this truly dreadful book, which is written in a shy-making faux-antique style that is presumably intended to evoke the Stoic philosophers who seem to represent Selbourne's main intellectual reference point. Dismissing Rawls and contemporary liberal theory in a sentence, he sets out his substantive claims as 'premises'. Premises are, of course, the sentences that, for purposes of argument, we treat as true in order to deduce other sentences from them. Selbourne certainly makes little effort to give us reasons for thinking his 'premises' to be true: what purports to be a philosophical treatise proves in fact to be a neo-conservative rant at the evils of decadent liberalism.

Despite the insouciance with which Giddens advocates overriding the liberties of the few in the alleged interest of the many, he doesn't go as far as Blair and Selbourne do when they assert the *priority* of duty over rights. He prefers the more moderate formula of what he calls 'the theorem "no rights without responsibilities"'.[44] Quite a lot of Selbourne's polemic in fact supports this weaker principle, that rights and duties are interdependent: 'while duties without rights make men slaves, rights without duties make men strangers to one another.'[45]

But there is an important sense in which *this* principle is just trivially true. To have a right is precisely to be in a position (morally and/or legally) to oblige others to respect one's exercise of that right. Thus, in one of the most important recent analyses of rights, Joseph Raz offers the following definition, ' "X has a right" if and only if X can have rights, and, other things being equal, an aspect of X's well-being (his interest) is a sufficient reason for holding some other person(s) to be under a duty.' Accordingly, '[r]ights are grounds of duties in others.'[46]

Contemporary philosophical discussion of rights is – for all the very real limitations of liberal political theory – a world away from the vulgar caricatures perpetrated by supporters of the Third Way and their neo-conservative allies. Let me mention merely two points. Even those philosophers – above all Rawls – who are accused by others (including Raz) of developing a 'rights-based morality' do not in fact treat rights as primordial. Thus for Rawls rights are to be assigned to individuals on the basis of the requirements of his two principles of justice. Raz's own view is that '[a]ssertions of rights are typically intermediate conclusions in arguments from ultimate values to duties.'[47] Rawls would dissent from this statement because of the reference to 'ultimate values', since he does not believe a liberal polity can legitimately base itself on any single substantive conception of the good. But rights occupy a similarly intermediate position in his own theory.[48]

Secondly, rights do not have to be given the kind of individualistic rendering that they have received both from classical liberals and from neo-conservatives such as Selbourne. Thus Raz argues that the ideal of personal autonomy – central to liberalism but also, as we have seen, shared by socialists, and supporters of the Third Way – requires that at least some collective goods are of intrinsic value: 'If having an autonomous life is an ultimate value, then having a sufficient range of options is of intrinsic value, for it is constitutive of an autonomous life that it is lived in circumstances where acceptable alternatives are present.' But the existence of such a range of options will itself depend upon social conditions some of which are collective goods – that is, '[g]eneral beneficial features of a society' from whose consumption no member of that society can be excluded.[49]

The foregoing should at least have succeeded in conveying something of the complexity of any serious account of rights. This does not mean that rights, whether individual or collective, are to be treated as absolute or indefeasible. Apart from all the issues raised by the possibility of rights conflicting, since rights (on Raz's account) derive from the interests of human beings, consideration of these interests is likely to identify circumstances where particular rights – or the rights of particular persons – should be overridden. But the classical liberals were right to this extent: restrictions on individual autonomy require principled *justification* – not just Giddens' airy maximizing over liberties or Selbourne's dogmatic assertion of the 'principle of duty'.

One might argue that New Labour authoritarianism is less

a matter of the rather flimsy theoretical rationalizations surveyed above than of civil liberties being one area where there is in fact considerable continuity with Old Labour. Traditionally Labour governments have not been particularly supportive of individual freedom. Roy Jenkins' famous tenure as a reforming Home Secretary in 1965–7, when abortion and homosexuality were legalized and theatre censorship scrapped, represents an exception rather the rule. Much more typical were Herbert Morrison's record during the 1940s and James Callaghan's in the late 1960s, when repressive pro-police and (in the latter case) anti-immigration policies were pursued.

But there is a much more recent precedent for the distinctive policy mix characteristic of New Labour – Thatcherism. Even before Mrs Thatcher took office in 1979 Stuart Hall pointed out that she stood for *laissez faire* in the economy and what he described as authoritarian populism in the social and political fields.[50] Andrew Gamble summed this up in the couplet 'free economy, strong state'.[51] But isn't this exactly the same basic recipe that we find in the Blair government – the further entrenchment and institutionalization of monetarist economics combined with moral authoritarianism?

There is, moreover, an important sense in which New Labour authoritarianism is a consequence of Gordon Brown's version of neo-liberal economics. Assuming (as Brown does) the basic truth of Friedman's conception of the economy, then, if macro-economic stability is secured and the right supply-side measures are in place, any further unemployment is voluntary. Unemployment is in these circumstances a consequence of the dysfunctional behaviour of individuals who refuse work, and this behaviour must in turn be caused either by their individual moral faults or by a more pervasive 'culture of poverty'. The kind of coercion implicit in the New Deal for the long-term unemployed, where government benefits are denied those refusing to take part, is therefore legitimate. So Brownite 'egalitarianism' dovetails in with Blairite authoritarianism.

None of the foregoing is intended to disparage the concept of community itself. Certainly anyone committed to achieving an egalitarian society has to take the concept very seriously indeed. G. A. Cohen has recently declared his sympathy for what he calls the 'old nostrum' that, '*for inequality to be overcome, there needs to be a revolution in feeling or motivation, as opposed to (just) in economic structures.*' He criticizes Rawls' interpretation of his second principle of justice, the difference principle, which allows social and economic inequalities only where these are necessary to benefit the worst off. For Rawls this authorizes the income differentials required to give the talented members of society the incentive to produce more, since the worst off will benefit from the higher output. This implies, Cohen argues, the co-existence of egalitarian structures with inegalitarian attitudes, at least on the part of the talented, since, if the latter accepted Rawls' principles of justice, they could not coherently demand special rewards for doing what comes naturally. Cohen concludes:

> A society that is just within the terms of the difference principle . . . requires not simply just coercive *rules*, but also an *ethos* of justice that informs individual choices. In the absence of such an ethos, inequalities will obtain that are not necessary to enhance the condition of the worse off: the required ethos promotes a distribution more just than what the rules of the economic game by themselves can secure. And what is indeed required is an ethos, a structure of response lodged in the motivations that inform everyday life.[52]

Plainly such a version of egalitarianism *requires* a strong conception of community according to which individuals produce to benefit one another, and not simply because of the expectation of material rewards. As Cohen stresses, such a motivation is inconsistent with a market economy, which relies instead on appeals to greed and fear.[53] This, then, is a socialist conception of community. There are, of course, many others. Indeed, one of the most powerful strands in contemporary Anglophone philosophy is what has come to be known as communitarianism, which criticizes liberal individualism for failing to take proper account of the larger social context on which both personal identity and ethical conceptions depend. But the most powerful version of communitarianism, developed by the Catholic philosopher Alasdair MacIntyre, is a critique not merely of liberalism, but of modernity *tout court* for shattering the ethical traditions represented by Aristotle's theory of the virtues and Augustinian Christianity.[54]

It is hard to see how the Third Way can mobilize any of these philosophical resources. It rejects the socialist critique of capitalism and embraces the market: 'we must never again be seen as anti-success, anti-competition, anti-profit, anti-markets,' Brown told British employers in November 1999.[55] New Labour has indeed gone considerably further than its Tory predecessors in promoting the corporate penetration of every aspect of social life.[56] It also engages in the facile celebration of modernity. Blair's speeches are littered with the word 'New' far beyond the limits of caricature. 'New, new, new. Everything is new,' he told the Congress of European Socialist Parties in June 1997.[57] His government coined the embarrassing slogan 'Cool Britannia' in order to associate itself with fashionable British artists, musicians, architects and designers – only to sink into the bathos of the Millennium Dome's tacky, down-at-heel modernism.

How can a political current so strongly identified with the forces of capitalism and modernity somehow attach itself to communitarian theories that define themselves in opposition to these forces? Certainly what has become Blair's cliché of 'Traditional Values in a Modern Setting' offers no easy solution to this problem. For one thing, there is no reason in principle why traditional values *should* survive. Take the concept of honour. As Montesquieu and Tocqueville showed, this is a virtue that plays a central role in aristocratic warrior societies. It may be the case that it still has something to say to us in modern capitalist societies, but this has to be demonstrated, through argument and practical example, not simply assumed. For another, important values may not be traditional. Equality, for example, the key to contemporary theories of justice, is not a traditional virtue, but a distinctively modern political ideal that emerged in the era of the English, American and French Revolutions.

It is tempting to see all the invocations of 'community' and affirmations of 'values' as a kind of kitsch, a 'caring' veneer pasted over the relentless commodification of the world that is the inner truth of the Third Way. Slavoj Žižek has targeted another aspect of the same phenomenon:

> This is the ultimate paradox we should bear in mind: today's prevailing 'psychologization' of social life (the deluge of psychological manuals from Dale Carnegie to John Gray, which all endeavour to convince us that the path to happy life is to be sought within us, in our psychic maturation and self-discovery; the Oprah Winfrey-style public confessions; the way in which politicians themselves render public their private traumas and concerns to justify political decisions) is the mask (or mode of appearance) of its *exact opposite*, of the growing disintegration of the proper 'psychological' dimension of authentic self-experience.[58]

Blair is a master of this confessional style of publicly expressing emotion as a signifier of sincerity – most famously, perhaps, on the occasion of Princess Diana's death in September 1997. A couple of months later he dealt with the scandal caused by the revelation that Bernie Ecclestone, the boss of Formula One, had given the Labour Party £1 million – a donation that critics were quick to connect with the government's decision to back-track on banning tobacco advertising in motor racing – by declaring on television: 'I am a pretty straight sort of a guy.'[59] Žižek comments on such performances:

> the public sharing of inner turmoil, the coincidence between public and private, even and especially when it is psychologically 'sincere', is cynical – not because such a public display of private doubts and uncertainties is faked, concealing true

privacy: what this display conceals is the *objective* socio-political and ideological dimension of the policies or decisions under discussion. The more this display is psychologically 'sincere', the more it is 'objectively' cynical in that it mystifies the true social meaning and effect of these policies or decisions.[60]

Some Third Way theorists are aware of the contradiction between embracing capitalism and affirming communitarian values. Charles Leadbeater, for example, dismisses community as a reactionary obstacle to the dynamic 'knowledge economy':

The communitarian critique of market capitalism is superficially appealing but eventually disappointing. Strong communities can be pockets of intolerance and prejudice. Settled, stable communities are the enemies of innovation, talent, creativity, diversity and experimentation. They are often hostile to outsiders, dissenters, young upstarts and immigrants. Community can too quickly become a rallying cry for nostalgia; that kind of community is the enemy of knowledge creation, which is the well-spring of economic growth.[61]

Giddens highlights the tension between tradition and modernity, and argues that this is pulling apart the neo-liberal combination of 'market fundamentalism and conservativism':

Devotion to the free market on the one hand, and to the traditional family and nation on the other, is self-contradictory. Individualism and choice are supposed to stop abruptly at the boundaries of the family and national identity, where tradition must stand intact. But nothing is more dissolving of tradition than the 'permanent revolution' of market forces. The dynamism of market societies undermines traditional structures of authority and fractures local communities; neo-liberalism creates new risks and uncertainties which it asks citizens simply to ignore. Moreover, it neglects the social basis of markets themselves, which depend upon the very communal forms that market fundamentalism indifferently throws to the winds.[62]

But precisely the same contradiction bisects New Labour. Blair is as solid a champion as Thatcher of Family, Church, Monarchy and Nation, albeit interpreting them in somewhat more contemporary terms; meanwhile, as we have seen, his government is guided by the same version of neo-liberal economics that she embraced. The instability in this kind of position was pointed out long before Giddens formulated his theory of 'late modernity'. Marx in the *Communist Manifesto* depicts capitalism as a revolutionary mode of production whose restless progress subverts traditional institutions and subjects the entire planet to its cycles of creative destruction. The apostles of the Third Way believe they can ride the tiger of global capitalism. They are likely to be disappointed.

3

Saviours of Humankind

3.1 Policing the world

J. G. Ballard in his latest novel, *Super-Cannes*, imagines a capitalist utopia, Eden-Olympia, a business park purpose-built in the hills above Cannes, the European capital of the New Economy where multinational executives work – and occasionally play – in lush, manicured, ultra-secure, high-tech seclusion. Conflict has been eliminated in this highly ordered, carefully designed community, 'where decisions about right and wrong were engineered into the social fabric, along with the fire drills and parking regulations'.[1] Inevitably the repressed returns, as bored senior executives in search of the authenticity of violence stage nocturnal raiding parties on Arab immigrants in the *bidonvilles* scattered along the Côte d'Azur.

This fantasy, while dramatizing some of Ballard's long-standing obsessions, offers an apt metaphor for contemporary capitalism – or at least for the self-image of that society to be found in Third Way thinking. Harmony reigns at the centre of the system, in the advanced capitalist countries, where, after the agonies of the twentieth century, enterprise and justice are in the process of being reconciled. Elsewhere, however, on the periphery, there are rogue and failing states still disfigured by tyranny and violence. So it is necessary from time to time for liberal capitalist societies to interrupt their affluent slumber and mount the police actions necessary to contain this disorder. Hence the various *ratissages* of the past decade – the Gulf War, the bombardments and blockades inflicted on Iraq and Yugoslavia, the expeditions to Somalia and Sierra Leone.

An important difference between Ballard's fiction and the real world concerns the motivations of the raiders. The liberal democracies do not mount their armed interventions driven by their own psychic needs. They also disclaim the geopolitical or economic aims that underlay the traditional *Realpolitik* of the bad old nineteenth and twentieth centuries. Rather they appeal to humanitarian principle – and, in the case of Third Way politicians, to the same values that motivate their domestic policies.

The decisive episode in this espousal of humanitarian warmaking was, of course, the 1999 Balkan War between NATO and Yugoslavia. The leaders of the NATO powers – chief among them Bill Clinton, Tony Blair, Lionel Jospin and Gerhard Schröder – sought to justify the NATO bombing campaign on the grounds that it was necessary to halt the Serb campaign of ethnic cleansing against the Albanian majority in Kosovo. But Blair went much further. In the first place, he proclaimed this to be a Third Way war, waged by 'a new generation of leaders in the United States and in Europe, who were born after World War II, who hail from the progressive side of politics, but who are prepared to be as firm as any of our predecessors right or left in seeing this thing through'.[2]

Secondly, Blair offered an ambitious rationalization of NATO policy through what amounted to an extension of Third Way doctrine to the international arena. 'This is a just war, based not on any territorial ambitions but on values.' Its justice sprang not merely from the plight of the victims of Serb aggression, but from the consequences of globalization, which 'is not just economic, it is also a political and security phenomenon'. Blair elaborated:

> We are witnessing the beginnings of a new doctrine of international community. By this I mean the explicit recognition that today more than ever before, we are mutually dependent, that national interest is to a significant extent governed by international collaboration and that we need a clear and coherent debate as to the direction that this doctrine takes us in each field of international endeavour. Just as within domestic politics, the notion of community – the belief that partnership and co-operation are essential to advance self-interest – is coming into its own; so it needs to find its international echo.[3]

Community is thus the master-concept on the international, as well as the national, level. This 'doctrine of the international community' implies, according to Blair, that the principle of non-interference implied by the notion of national sovereignty can, in certain circumstances, be overriden. He set out 'five major considerations' that should guide decisions by the Great Powers over whether or not to intervene – the necessity of armed force, the exhaustion of diplomatic options, the feasibility of military operations, the intervening states' willingness to make a long-term commitment, and the involvement of their national interests in the conflict in question.[4] Confident that the Kosovan case met these criteria, Blair announced at the end of the war: 'good has triumphed over evil, justice has overcome barbarism, and the values of civilization have prevailed.'[5]

Others were, of course, more sceptical about the justice of this 'war for values'. Blair himself acknowledged: 'Looking around the world there are many regimes that are undemocratic and engaged in barbarous acts. If we wanted to right every wrong that we see in the modern world then we would do little else than intervene in the affairs of other countries.'[6] So why was Slobodan Milošević's Serb nationalist regime picked out for special attention? Critics were quick to point out that comparable atrocities to those for which Milošević was responsible in Kosovo were being committed by other states – for example, Turkey and Colombia. The regimes controlling these countries were, furthermore, likely to be amenable to outside pressure given their dependence on Western support. But this support was indicative of their importance to Western interests, which in turn offers a *prima facie* explanation why Turkey and Colombia were not selected for the treatment meted out to Yugoslavia.[7]

Defenders of the Balkan War sought to drown out such irritating quibbles by pointing to the massacres and expulsions of Kosovo Albanians by Serb forces. Constant comparisons between these atrocities and the Nazi Holocaust were used to shut off debate. At the start of the bombing campaign Clinton said: 'it's about our values. What if someone had listened to Winston Churchill and stood up to Adolph [*sic*] Hitler earlier. How many lives might have been saved?'[8] This analogy's persuasive effect was strengthened by guilty memories especially strong in Western left-liberal circles of earlier atrocities committed by Serb nationalist forces during the Bosnian War – most notably the massacre of some 7,000 Bosnian Muslims at Srebrenica in July 1995. It was further reinforced by the claim that an even greater slaughter was unfolding in Kosovo.

Typical of the bullying style in which this argument was made is this attack by one of the more assiduous atrocity-hunters, John Sweeney, on three leading British critics of the war – the journalist John Pilger, the playwright Harold Pinter and the writer and broadcaster Tariq Ali: 'All these atrocities have one thing in common. They are the collateral damage of Milošević. And Kosovo, when we open the mass graves, will be the worst. Pilger, Pinter and Ali will be shamed as corpse after corpse is dug up, tens of thousands of them.'[9]

Embarrassingly for Sweeney and his ilk, when the graves were opened after the NATO occupation of Kosovo in June 1999, the bodies exhumed did not number 'tens of thousands', let alone the hundreds of thousands sometimes hinted at by NATO leaders. 'The final number of bodies uncovered will be less than 10,000 and probably more accurately determined as between two and three thousand,' a spokesman for the International Criminal Tribunal for the former Yugoslavia said in August 2000.[10] This is further evidence of the criminal nature of the Milošević regime, but to compare Serb atrocities in Kosovo to the Holocaust is to trivialize the all too genuine cases of genocide witnessed by the twentieth century. It is clear that the main aim of the killings actually committed by Milošević's forces was part of a concerted effort to drive the Albanians out of Kosovo. But defenders of the war have still to prove that this – once again, undeniably criminal – operation would have occurred without the NATO bombing campaign rather than in response to it. In a highly critical analysis of the conduct of the war, the House of Commons Select Committee on Defence commented: 'It was unwise for politicians to either have thought, or ever suggested, that a humanitarian disaster, which by 24 March 1999 was already underway, could be *averted* from the air. On the contrary, all the evidence suggests that plans to initiate the air campaign hastened the onset of the disaster.'[11]

Scepticism about the NATO case was further reinforced by examination of the ill-named Rambouillet Accords, Yugoslav refusal to accept which had been the immediate occasion of the conflict. The terms of this ultimatum – for example, the notorious Annexe B, which gave NATO forces unlimited access to the whole of Yugoslavia – seemed calculated to invite Milošević's rejection. The American Secretary of State, Madeleine Albright, admitted as much after the war was over. Clinton, in the speech already cited above, offered a very different rationale from all the talk about fighting for 'the values of civilization':

> Now, if we have learned anything after the Cold War, and our memories of World War II, it is that if our country is going to be prosperous and secure, we need a Europe that is safe, secure, free, united, a good partner with us for trading; they're wealthy enough to buy our products; and someone

who will share the burdens of taking care of the problems of the world. . . . *Now, that's what this Kosovo thing is all about.*[12]

These remarkably frank observations suggest that geopolitical rather than humanitarian considerations loomed large in American planning. Clinton himself also made the connection with NATO's expansion into East-Central Europe, which took effect a few weeks after the outbreak of the war, in April 1999. NATO expansion, as we shall see in the rest of this chapter, was part of a larger strategy to maintain US hegemony throughout the Eurasian continent. In this context, precipitating a brief police action in Kosovo must have recommended itself to the State Department officials who appear to have been the chief architects of the war as an easy object lesson in the new NATO's capacity to project its power against recalcitrant states.

In the event, of course, things went badly wrong. Rather than promptly capitulate, as Albright and her advisers seem to have expected he would, Milošević unleashed the horrors of ethnic cleansing on the Kosovo Albanians. To avoid a ground offensive against Kosovo, and the high NATO casualties this would probably have entailed, Clinton was forced, through the Schröder government's good offices, to open a channel to the Russians.[13] When finally persuaded by Moscow that he was internationally isolated, Milošević accepted a deal that, if it had been on offer at Rambouillet, would almost certainly have made the war unnecessary. The Yugoslav army emerged from its hiding places to withdraw from Kosovo with its numbers, weaponry and morale intact, and hunkered down along the border in readiness for the next round. The fate of Kosovo under NATO occupation is well summarized by the neo-conservative commentator Edward Luttwak:

All that been achieved . . . is the replacement of Serbian ethnic cleansing with Albanian ethnic cleansing and of Serbian misrule with the collective misrule of a UN/NATO/EU protectorate that is conspicuously failing to provide day-to-day security, or the wherewithal of economic reconstruction, or a framework for the emergence of some sort of civilized politics.[14]

3.2 The armature of hegemony

The Kosovo débâcle did not diminish the enthusiasm of the New Labour government at least for humanitarian intervention. Blair was the most belligerent of the NATO leaders, campaigning for a ground war in Kosovo. Thwarted in this desire, he nevertheless regularly cited the conflict as one of his government's great successes, though it wasn't always clear how much this was as an instance of humanitarian intervention or as evidence of his toughness – as in the memorandum cited in §2.3 above: Kosovo thus functioned as his version of the Falklands War, which proved that Mrs Thatcher indeed deserved the title 'Iron Lady'. Blair in any case authorized in May 2000 the dispatch of troops to intervene in the civil war raging in the diamond-rich former British colony of Sierra Leone.

Supporters of the Third Way sympathetic to such interventions – at least when they can be plausibly described as humanitarian – would no doubt find the deflationary analysis of the Balkan War offered in the preceding section, which detects geopolitical considerations behind humanitarian professions, an example of 'old' thinking still rooted in the European system with its perpetual rivalries and wars and in that system's extension during the era of superpower competition after 1945.

From the perspective of the Third Way, fundamental conflicts of interest among states are becoming a thing of the past. Giddens calls the contemporary liberal-democratic state 'the state without enemies'.[15] He declares that 'the older forms of geopolitics are becoming obsolete. Although this is a contentious point, I would say that, following the dissolving of the Cold War, most nations no longer have enemies. Who are the enemies of Britain, or France, or Brazil?'[16]

On the face of it, this is a strange question to ask, since France and Britain took part in two wars in the decade after 1989 – the 1991 Gulf War against Iraq and the 1999 Balkan War against Yugoslavia. But contemporary Western doctrine has come up with a classification of states that can accommodate these counter-examples. This contrasts the liberal democracies, which are united in such strong bonds of shared values and interests that war among them is now inconceivable, with, on the one hand, 'rogue states' (recently renamed by the State Department 'states of concern') that fail to respect the norms of the international community, and, on the other hand, 'failing states' incapable of providing their citizens with the minimum conditions of social cohesion. Both these categories of non-liberal states are the legitimate objects of outside intervention: from time to time police actions may be required against rogue states such as Iraq, Yugoslavia or North Korea, while 'failing states' may need rescue by the international community.

This classification has found its philosophical mirror in John Rawls' *The Law of Peoples*. This identifies four principal kinds of societies: liberal peoples – constitutional democracies governed on the basis of some member of the family of liberal conceptions of justice; 'decent peoples', whose social structure is hierarchical but which allow their members some participation in public life through a 'decent consultation hierarchy' (Rawls seems to have in mind here traditional Islamic polities); 'outlaw states', which still regard war as a legitimate instrument of policy; and 'burdened societies', whose unfavourable circumstances prevent them from attaining the status of either a liberal or a decent society.

Liberal and decent peoples both constitute cases of 'well-ordered peoples' capable, thanks to the level of co-operation they have achieved domestically, of forming a Society of Peoples whose members renounce the use of war against each other and consent to be governed by certain 'familiar principles and traditional principles of justice' that together constitute the Law of Peoples. But one of these principles – the duty of non-intervention – 'will obviously have to be qualified in the general case of outlaw states and grave violations of human rights. Although suitable for a society of well-ordered peoples, it fails in the case of a society of disordered peoples in which wars and serious violations of human rights are endemic.' Thus it is in principle 'legitimate to interfere with outlaw states simply because they violate human rights'.[17]

Rawls concedes that his normative account of constitutional democracy may not correspond to the actual behaviour of liberal states: 'The possibility of democratic peace is not incompatible with *actual* democracies – being marked, as they are, by considerable injustice, oligarchic tendencies, and monopolistic interests – intervening, often covertly, in smaller and weaker countries, and even in less well-established democracies.'[18] But the general thrust of *The Law of Peoples* is to minimize the gap between philosophical norm and political reality. Thus Rawls resists proposals to extend his difference principle – according to which, inequalities should only be tolerated where they are to the advantage of the worst off – from the structure of individual societies to that of the entire world. He prefers to such a cosmopolitan conception of justice, which would entail considerable redistribution on a global scale, the much more modest Duty of Assistance to 'burdened societies'.[19]

Rawls seems to have been encouraged to envisage a relatively close fit between norm and reality by certain historical experiences – notably '[t]he absence of war among major established democracies', which he says 'is as close as anything we know to a simple empirical regularity in relations among peoples', and the 'basic and historically profound changes in how the powers of sovereignty have been conceived since World War II'.[20] Here Rawls' philosophical conception of the Law of Peoples joins more empirical theories of political globalization.

Such a theory is most systematically presented by David Held, Anthony McGrew and their colleagues. They argue that the old system of sovereign states brought into being in Europe by the Treaty of Westphalia of 1648 is being replaced by what they call 'global politics':

Traditional conceptions of state sovereignty and autonomy are being renegotiated and rearticulated within the changing processes and structures of regional and global order. States, moreover, are being locked into complex overlapping political domains – what we earlier referred to as multilateral governance. Thus national sovereignty and national autonomy have to be thought of as embedded within broader frameworks of governance in which they have become but one set of principles among others underlying the exercise of political authority. The Westphalian regime of state sovereignty and state autonomy is undergoing a significant alteration as it becomes qualified in a fundamental way.[21]

More specifically, '[n]ational government is locked into an array of global, regional and multilateral systems of governance.' These 'forms of global governance' embrace formally institutionalized systems of international or regional co-operation such as the UN, the WTO, NATO and the EU; they also include the more informal networks constituted by multinational companies, 'transnational social movements' and non-governmental organizations, the international regimes that have evolved to regulate different aspects of international relations, and the emerging elements of 'cosmopolitan law', notably 'human rights law . . ., the law of war, the law governing war crimes and crimes against humanity, and environmental law'. The net result of these innovations is 'a deterritorialization of political authority', although the authors concede that the extent and implications of this process remain at least partially indeterminate.[22]

The critical issue raised by political globalization concerns the impact of these forms of governance on the distribution of power: do they represent the progressive transcendence of an inter-state system primarily regulated by the conflicting interests among the major powers? There are good reasons for doubting this. Held, McGrew and their collaborators enthusiastically list the 'regulatory regimes' established from the second half of the nineteenth century onwards 'for, in principle, the predictable and orderly conduct of pressing transnational processes'.[23] But the formation by 1914 of bodies such as the International Telegraphic Union, the International Bureau of Commercial Statistics or the International Geodetic Association did not prevent the state-system from descending into unprecedented barbarity during the era of the two world wars.

There has, as the co-authors note, been a further, very rapid proliferation of international organizations since 1945, a process intensified by the higher profile of multilateral co-operation ushered in by the end of the Cold War: for example, the formal extension of the G-7 group of leading industrial powers to include Russia; the replacement of GATT with the much stronger and more interventionist World Trade Organization; the final achievement of European economic and monetary union with the launch of the euro in January 1999; the development of other forms of interregional co-operation such as the North American Free Trade Agreement and the Asia-Pacific Economic Forum; UN-authorized military interventions in a variety of countries; and the expansion of NATO into East-Central Europe.

But the mere fact of institutional proliferation tells us nothing about the actual relations of power that subsist among these networks of 'global governance'. To a large extent the institutions and regimes welcomed by Held, McGrew and their colleagues as the avatars of 'cosmopolitan democracy' have served further to institutionalize the American hegemony. The co-authors' discussion of hegemony is, at best, confused. Thus they write that, 'despite its potential for global hegemony following the end of the Cold War, the US has abandoned any pretensions to global empire or overt hegemony since its enormous structural power has remained deeply inscribed into the nature and functioning of the present world order.'[24]

There seem to be two thoughts here: first, the United States does not rely on the kind of formal imperial institutions used by earlier leading powers such as Spain, France or Britain, which is true enough not merely of the period since 1989, but of the entire postwar era; secondly, it does not need such institutions since the operation of the existing global order is structurally biased in its favour. This also is true, but it implies that the US is, in effect if not in name, globally hegemonic. This is, however, contradicted by a passage on the next page that is worth quoting at length because it reflects the widespread hope that political globalization represents a genuine diffusion of power on a world scale:

> the intensification of economic globalization has been associated with an intensification of global economic surveillance, enhanced supervisory activity and the deepening of international regulatory activity, for instance through the WTO. The deregulation of national economies has been accompanied by new forms of regulation in the global domain. Yet these developments did not receive a boost while US power was at its apogee, but while it experienced relative decline. In this context, the present era may be distinguished from the past in so far as the rhythm of globalization appears no longer to be correlated with the rise and decline of a single hegemonic power or bloc. . . . Contemporary patterns of economic globalization reflect a cumulative tendency, in the context of new multilateral structures of regulation and control, towards more self-organizing and market-driven arrangements, which tend only to receive overt political direction from a hegemonic power at times of crisis.[25]

So, either the US is a declining power, or it has nobly renounced its 'potential for global hegemony', preferring to assert its underlying strength only at moments of crisis. This is, to say the least, less than clear. Held, McGrew and their co-authors refer in support of their argument to Robert O. Keohane's book *After Hegemony*. This is concerned with exploring the limits of what is known among scholars of international relations as the theory of hegemonic stability. This asserts that (1) 'order in world politics is typically created by a single dominant power,' and (2) 'the maintenance of order requires continued hegemony.'[26]

Keohane's main reference point is Kenneth N. Waltz's celebrated restatement of the Realist tradition in international relations, which explains world politics as in large part the consequence of a structure of competing states conceived as self-interested rational actors.[27] Despite the anarchic character of such systems, this theory predicts a high degree of international stability so long as changes in the distribution of economic and military power do not give individual states an incentive to seek the transformation of the system: such disequilibria have typically been resolved by 'hegemonic wars' waged to change the entire international structure.[28]

From the standpoint of this theory the late twentieth century presented a threatening aspect. By the 1970s at the latest, US hegemony appeared to be on the wane. Militarily, the Soviet Union had developed the capacity to project its power globally by conventional as well as nuclear means. Economically, the US was in relative decline compared to Japan and West Germany. If Charles Kindleberger's influential interpretation of the Great Depression of the 1930s were correct, this was an especially dangerous situation. According to Kindleberger, the slump reflected the fact that there was no hegemonic power to provide the public goods – in particular the liquidity necessary to stabilize panicky financial markets – on which international economic stability depended: Britain could no longer play this role and the US was unwilling to. The global monetary disorder that developed in the late 1960s suggested that history was in the process of repeating itself.[29]

Keohane challenged such prognoses by pointing to the relative stability of various international economic regimes – for example, those concerned with money, oil and trade – despite the decline in US power. A hegemonic state might initiate such regimes, but once established they could develop a self-sustaining quality. States might find it in their interests to engage in institutionalized co-operation even when not coerced to do so, since international regimes offered various benefits by, for example, reducing uncertainty and transaction costs. These considerations demonstrated the fact that hegemony is not a necessary condition of international stability; they also highlighted the necessity of going beyond the kind of rational choice theory used by Waltz. Institutions had an effectivity of their own irreducible to the self-interested calculations of actors. Accordingly, '[a] synthesis of Realism and Institutionalism is necessary.'[30]

Keohane offers a theoretically rigorous, and empirically supported, analysis. It suffers, however, from one obvious defect, namely that it relies on a factual premiss that is false. Rumours of the demise of American hegemony have been much exaggerated. US relative decline in the 1960s and 1970s was a reality, but the extrapolations made from this have proved to be unreliable. Properly to understand the extent and the limits of this decline requires considering the broader history of the international system since 1945. The best theoretical framework in which to understand this history remains, in my view, that developed during the First World War by Nikolai Bukharin, who argued that modern imperialism is characterized by two fundamental, and partially contradictory, tendencies – towards, on the one hand, the global integration of capital and, on the other, the interweaving of economic and geopolitical competition in the international system of states.[31]

Between 1945 and 1990 world politics had a bipolar structure reflecting the effective partition of the globe between the two rival superpower blocs. In the West, this involved the integration of the leading capitalist states under US political, military and economic leadership. In Keohane's words: 'In the shelter of its military strength, the United States constructed a liberal capitalist world political economy based on multilateral principles and embodying rules that the United States approved.'[32] This was true of the institutions of the so-called 'Bretton Woods System' – the International Monetary Fund, the World Bank, GATT, etc. – but also of the NATO military alliance.

One consequence of this state of affairs was the partial dissociation of economic and geopolitical competition. During the era of classical imperialism – roughly 1870–1945 – economic and politico-military rivalries tended to be mutually reinforcing. In both world wars, access to the resources necessary to sustain economic and military expansion was a major strategic consideration, especially for challengers to the existing international structure such as Germany and Japan. This changed after 1945. The leading antagonists of 1914–18 and 1939–45 were, with the exception of Russia and China, integrated into the same politico-military bloc under American leadership. Within the framework of the Bretton Woods institutions, they could pursue their economic rivalries without this producing the kind of geopolitical tensions that helped to precipitate the world wars.

It is against this background that American firms began to find themselves under a growing competitive disadvantage vis-à-vis their Japanese and German competitors. Even during the Long Boom of the 1950s and 1960s – the fabled 'Golden Age' of world capitalism – the US economy grew much more slowly than those in continental Europe and Japan.[33] Relative American economic decline became perceptible from the mid-1960s onwards and was reflected in monetary instability and the intensification of international competition. But, though political tensions among the major Western economies grew – for example, after the 'Nixon shock' of August 1971 when Washington abandoned the gold exchange standard as a prelude to devaluing the dollar – the US retained its leading position.[34]

It was the experience of the international economic conflicts of the 1960s and 1970s that led commentators to announce the end of American hegemony. But the 1980s produced a very different outcome. In the first place, brutal economic restructuring allowed US firms substantially to increase their competitiveness compared to their Japanese and European rivals.[35] Secondly, the Soviet Union entered a protracted economic and political crisis that led to its collapse and that of its system of satellite states in Eastern and Central Europe. This left the US as overwhelmingly the dominant military power on a world scale: by 1996 the American defence budget was slightly larger than the combined military spending of Russia, Japan, France, Germany, Britain and China.[36]

As the Cold War came to a close Joseph Nye therefore argued that the US remained the leading power, outdistancing other states in its command both of traditional power sources (natural resources, the military, economy and technology) and of the 'soft power' that derives from the global influence of American culture.[37] It is, however, important to see that the great turning point of 1989–91 was a moment of potential threat to US hegemony. The pressures of economic competition were already tending partially to disaggregate the Western bloc. The end of the Cold War threatened to take this process further.

During the so-called 'Second Cold War' of the late 1970s and early 1980s the US had sought to use what was perceived to be a greater Soviet military threat to reassert its leading political role in Europe. But the disintegration of the USSR removed the geopolitical restraints that had helped to keep American allies/rivals such as Japan and West Germany in place. In particular a re-unified Germany began to assert itself on the world stage – for example, in July 1990 Chancellor Helmut Kohl settled the question of its membership of NATO through bilateral negotiations with Moscow, confronting Washington with a *fait accompli*, and in December 1991 his Foreign Minister, Hans-Dietrich Genscher, sabotaged the Bush administration's efforts to keep Yugoslavia together by forcing through a European Community decision to recognize Slovenia and Croatia as independent states.

Concerted and sustained efforts were required in order to reassert the leading politico-military role of the US. The 1991 Gulf War provided an opportunity to remind Germany and Japan that the security of their oil supplies depended ultimately on American armed might. The UN-sanctioned Coalition that was constructed to drive Iraqi forces out of Kuwait indicated the potential for multilateral bodies to provide a legitimizing and mobilizing framework for US-led initiatives. Sometimes these involved *ad hoc* efforts: thus the G-7 rescue package for Mexico after the 1994 financial crash involved Germany and Britain (much to their disgust) paying heavily to indemnify American investors for their rash speculation in what had seemed to be a particularly attractive 'emerging market'.

A number of factors facilitated the reassertion of US leadership. Japan during the 1990s experienced the most serious and protracted economic slump suffered by an advanced country since the 1930s. For Germany also the decade was, for the most part, a period of prolonged economic stagnation. The contrast with the booming American economy indicated for many the superiority of the Anglo-Saxon free-market model of capitalism. The European Union, newly strengthened by the 1991 Maastricht Treaty, nevertheless proved unable to cope with the disintegration of Yugoslavia. American military muscle and political leadership were required to bring the Bosnian War to an end, setting the pattern for the 1999 crisis over Kosovo. By the late 1990s, Zbigniew Brzezinski, National Security Assistant to President Jimmy Carter and one of the architects of NATO expansion, could write: 'The brutal fact is that Western Europe, and increasingly also Central Europe, remains largely an American protectorate, with its allied states reminiscent of ancient vassals and tributaries.'[38]

NATO expansion reflected the scale of US ambitions. It implied the transformation of a defensive Western European military alliance into a geopolitical bloc stretching far into the Eurasian continent. The inclusion of Poland, Hungary and the Czech Republic took NATO to the borders of the old USSR. Among the countries lined up as candidate members of the alliance through Partnership for Peace agreements were a plethora of former Soviet republics extending into Central Asia. The intensity of American interest in this area was reflected in the presence at NATO's fiftieth anniversary celebrations in April 1999 of the five ex-Soviet republics – Georgia, Ukraine, Uzbekistan, Azerbaijan and Moldova – forming a new pro-Western alliance, GUUAM.

The reinvention of NATO served three strategic aims. First, it secured Russia's encirclement far more effectively than anything the US had been able to achieve during the Cold War. Ukraine acquired a pivotal importance, reflecting the fact that its independence severely limited Russia's ability to assert itself as a European power: as Brzezinski puts it, '[w]ithout Ukraine, Russia ceases to be a Eurasian empire.'[39] Hence the special attention devoted to Ukraine – for example, generous US aid and a meeting of NATO's supreme body, the North Atlantic Council, in Kiev in March 2000.[40]

Secondly, the expanding NATO provided the institutional framework through which access by the Western powers in general and the US in particular could be guaranteed to the crucial Caspian Sea zone, rich in oil and natural gas deposits, and strategically sited between Russia and China. Thirdly, NATO's new 'strategic concept', with the scope it gave for 'out-of-area' operations usually mounted for humanitarian reasons, legitimized Western military interventions in which the US could, where appropriate, play the predominant role. The Kosovo War was, as I suggested in §3.1 above, a test-case for such operations, providing, among other things, a precedent for military interventions to be carried out unilaterally by NATO where the necessary authority would not be forthcoming from a UN Security Council on which Russia and China still wielded their vetos.[41]

The case of NATO expansion indicates that the belief, expressed by Held, McGrew and their co-authors, that contemporary globalization involves the growing predominance of genuinely 'multilateral structures of regulation and control' needs to be treated with considerable scepticism. These authors are preoccupied particularly with forms of economic regulation (indeed their discussion of 'military globalization' rather economistically focuses on patterns of trade and production rather than the changing forms of geopolitical competition[42]). But even here the picture hardly resembles anything that can be described as genuine multilateralism.

The 'Washington consensus' of privatization, deregulation and liberalization enforced on Third World and ex-Stalinist countries by the IMF and the World Bank very much reflects these institutions' close links with the US Treasury. During the Asian crisis of 1997–8, when IMF austerity programmes were imposed on Thailand, South Korea and Indonesia (in the last case helping to precipitate a popular rising), the Fund's managing director, Michel Camdessus, declared: 'What we are doing coincides with the basic purposes of American diplomacy in the world.'[43] This followed a successful campaign by the Clinton administration to block a Japanese proposal for the establishment of an Asian Monetary Fund to deal with the crisis. Such an innovation might have impeded one of the main aims of the IMF plans – to open up the nationally organized economies of East Asia characterized by close links between local capital and the state and thereby to facilitate multinational investment.[44]

Held, McGrew and their collaborators cite the WTO as a case of 'the deepening of international regulatory activity'. Indeed it is, but in whose interests? The principal function of the WTO appears to be twofold: first, to provide a more effective forum than the old GATT in which the major trading powers – the so-called 'Quad' of the US, the EU, Japan and Canada, along with the Cairns group of leading agricultural exporters – can prosecute their disputes; secondly, to provide a much more rigorous enforcement mechanism for imposing decisions broadly favourable to the Washington consensus. While disputes panels have occasionally found against the US, the general framework in which the WTO operates is biased strongly in favour of the Anglo-American free-market model.[45] Sometimes the bias is a lot cruder: the WTO summit collapsed in Seattle at the beginning of December 1999 not simply because of the mass demonstrations outside, but also because of the arrogance with which US Trade Representative Charlene Barshevsky sought to present Southern delegates with a series of *faits accomplis* agreed by the leading Western powers during private discussions conducted in the 'green room'.[46]

None of the foregoing is intended to deny the important and relatively disinterested work done by a variety of specialized international agencies and NGOs. Nor, as I argue in the following section, can the existing global order be seen as merely a tool of Washington. But the current functioning of the leading international institutions – the UN itself, the

IMF/World Bank, the WTO, NATO, etc. – can only be understood in the context of the reassertion of US power that I have tried briefly to document here. The transformation of the Organization for Security and Co-operation in Europe – set up during the Cold War at Soviet behest and intended to provide a negotiating framework that transcended the partition of the continent – into an instrument of American policy in the Balkans during the late 1990s is as good a symbol as any of this process.[47] To ignore it, as theorists of political globalization do, is simply jejune.

3.3 Imperial collisions

Zbigniew Brzezinski not long ago sought to formulate what one might call the Grand Strategy of the American Empire in the twenty-first century. Disdaining euphemism, he set out the realities of 'global governance':

> The collapse of its rival left the United States in a unique position. It became simultaneously the first and the only global power. And yet America's global supremacy is reminiscent in some ways of earlier empires, notwithstanding their more confined regional scope. These empires based their power on a hierarchy of vassals, tributaries, protectorates, and colonies, with those on the outside generally viewed as barbarians. To some degree, that anachronistic terminology is not altogether inappropriate for some of the states currently within the American orbit.[48]

American primacy is for Brzezinski less a matter simply of the resources at Washington's command than of its ability to dominate the Eurasian continent, home to two of the world's three most productive regions and six of the seven major military powers. The major threats to US hegemony come from the possibility of a Russo-Chinese alliance against the West, and from the sheer instability of the 'Eurasian Balkans', the zone stretching from the actual Balkans and the Near East deep into Central Asia that separates the prosperous western and eastern tips of the continent and may soon become one of their main sources of energy. The EU, Brzezinski argues, is critical to US capacity to manage these and other potential dangers:

Europe is America's geopolitical bridgehead on the Eurasian continent. America's geostrategic stake in Europe is enormous . . . the Atlantic alliance entrenches American political influence and military power directly on the Eurasian mainland. At this stage of American–European relations, with the allied European nations still highly dependent on US security protection, any expansion in the scope of Europe becomes automatically an expansion in the scope of direct US influence as well. Conversely, without close transatlantic ties, America's primacy in Eurasia promptly fades away. US control over the Atlantic Ocean and the ability to project influence and power deeper into Eurasia would be severely circumscribed.[49]

The expansion of the complex of European institutions – critically both the EU and NATO – accordingly represents for Brzezinski the extension of American influence, as well as, as we have already seen, a means of containing any revival of Russian power. But this is part of a larger 'geostrategy' whose objective is to maintain US hegemony using both the classic imperial methods of divide-and-rule and a network of alliances and partnerships designed to lock potential challengers into an international system orchestrated from Washington:

In the short run, it is in America's interest to consolidate and perpetuate the prevailing geopolitical pluralism on the map of Eurasia. That puts a premium on maneuver and manipulation in order to prevent the emergence of a hostile coalition that would eventually seek to challenge America's primacy, not to mention the remote possibility of any one particular state seeking to do so. By the middle term [the next twenty years or so], *the foregoing should gradually yield to a greater emphasis on the emergence of increasingly important but strategically compatible partners who, prompted by American leadership, might help to shape a more co-operative trans-*

Eurasian security system. Eventually, in the much longer run still, the foregoing could phase into a global core of genuinely shared political responsibility.[50]

The replacement of American primacy by a genuinely multilateral arrangement, even among the Great Powers, is thus put off into a future too remote to figure in any serious calculations. Brzezinski is refreshingly free from the cant normally used by Western governments and their advisers when discussing international politics. Martin Wight described what he called 'the radical ambiguity of a position like that of the Western powers after 1919, who after a successful career as burglars tried to settle down as country-gentlemen making intermittent appearances at the magistrate's bench'.[51] Hypocrisy would be a less charitable way of characterizing this stance. At least Brzezinski is free of that. His analysis has two further merits. First, he highlights the respects in which the strengthening of international institutions does not necessarily threaten, but may indeed reinforce, American hegemony. Secondly, he highlights that this primacy does arise automatically, but needs to be sustained by concerted efforts directed especially at maintaining 'the prevailing geopolitical pluralism on the Eurasian continent' – that is, to keep potential challengers divided and therefore relatively weak.

This second point alerts us to an ambiguity in the term 'hegemony'. It can be interpreted as the kind of absolute political domination at least theoretically exercised by the rulers of the ancient empires.[52] Alternatively and more usefully, hegemony may be understood in much more relative terms: here it involves the use of a variety of methods – coercion, persuasion, bribery, alliances, the impersonal functioning of economic mechanisms, etc. – by the most powerful state to secure its objectives in an international system where other players have the ability to impede or frustrate the hegemon's initiatives and, in certain circumstances, even to challenge it altogether.[53] This helps to explain Washington's reliance on multilateral institutions: bodies such as the G-7, the IMF, the WTO and NATO serve both to allow the US to mobilize the support and resources of the Western powers behind its initiatives and to provide bargaining forums within which conflicts of interest among the leading capitalist states can be articulated and regulated in relatively non-disruptive ways.

These considerations are important because they highlight the fact that, despite the reality of US hegemony, we do not live in a world where all other powers lie prostrate before US 'ultra-imperialism'. Perry Anderson has argued that the Kosovo War demonstrated US ability to see off potential challengers – Russia reduced to 'a token auxiliary', China willing to ignore the destruction of its Belgrade embassy because 'it had made clear that nothing will be allowed to disturb good relations with Washington.'[54] While it is true that the Clinton administration was able in the short term to neutralize China and Russia, and indeed to use the latter to persuade Milošević to come to settlement, the longer-term consequences of the Balkan War are more likely to lead these two states and other states to form coalitions aimed at containing American power.

Thus the security consultants Stratfor argue that

> the West's decision to bomb Iraq in December 1998 – followed by the war in Kosovo, both in direct opposition to Russian wishes – generated a revolution in Russian policy. These two actions convinced the Russians that the United States intended to reduce Russia to the status of a tertiary power. Washington's systematic indifference to Russian wishes convinced the Russian national security community that without leverage against the United States, Russia would have no traction whatsoever. Economic relations with the West had effectively collapsed in the financial crisis of August 1998, so the Russians felt they had little to lose.[55]

Certainly Russian policy under Vladimir Putin – notably his reversal of Russia's promise never to use nuclear weapons first and explicit adoption of a strategic doctrine aimed at countering 'hegemonic' power – indicated Moscow's increasingly antagonistic stance towards the US. China's rapid arms build-up, reflecting the Beijing regime's desire to assert itself as a regional and eventually a world power and to recover the lost province of Taiwan, also brought it potentially into conflict with the US. The *Financial Times* described a Defense Department assessment of China's ability to retake Taiwan by force as 'one of very few US government documents in recent years that have described the potential for future military rivalry between China and the US'.[56] For America's part, the size of the military establishment maintained by the Pentagon in the post-Cold War era is explicable only on the assumption that US planners believe it necessary to prepare for possible wars with both Russia and China.[57]

Deploying the same kind of Realist analysis that informs Brzezinski's survey of world politics, Stratfor views the current international scene from the perspective of the 'unchanging pattern of great power competition' over the past 500 years:

> the past ten years did not constitute the end of history. They were simply an interregnum, like so many others before it, in which the victory of a single power or coalition could appear to be so complete that the emergence of a new challenge to that power was unthinkable. America's victory over the Soviet Union was so stunning, unexpected and absolute that it seemed that American values were now global values and that American power was now absolute. However, no set of values is ever global, and no nation's power, no matter how great, is ever absolute. . . . The game of nations is not over.[58]

Stratfor describes the emerging international structure as based on 'a three-player game between the United States, China and Russia'. This is not the same as 'a new Cold War'.[59] The Cold War involved a sharply polarized world divided between two antagonistic blocs to which most states of any significance belonged. The differences in economic and military capabilities between the US and the two main challenger powers, Russia and China, make such a polarization improbable. More likely is 'coalition-building, designed to constrain the United States' by 'increasing the probability of attracting American attention and generating sufficient threats to force favorable policy shifts in Washington'.[60]

The result is a highly fluid state of affairs, in which, precisely because US pre-eminence allows Washington to remain indifferent to many issues, secondary powers can increase their influence through shifting alliances. France's complex foreign policy since the 1950s, designed to remain part of the Western bloc while seeking a variety of ploys – European integration, an African neo-colonial empire, bilateral relations with post-Stalinist Russia – to counter-balance US power, is likely to be a model for many other states:

> the secondary powers are themselves near great powers. . . . Any one of them can make the decision to enter the first rank, behind only the United States, if they choose. That means that as the new epoch matures, the three-player game can rapidly acquire new players. Some of them will not come from the traditional quarters. India or Turkey, for example, might evolve over time. The important point is that the structure of the three-player game increases the incentive for secondary powers to emulate France and, in so doing, increases the probability of an increase in the ranks of great powers.
>
> That may make for a more unstable world. It will certainly make for a more complex one.[61]

Stratfor cheerfully describes the structure of world politics as a game, just as Brzezinski calls Eurasia a chessboard, around which Washington can move the pieces of its grand strategy. These metaphors indicate the characteristic moral indifference with which Realists analyse the process of geo-political competition that, at best, wastes on the military vast resources better employed elsewhere and at worst inflicts terrible carnage and suffering on the victims of Great-Power conflict. The analytical flaws of Realism are also well known: it fails to acknowledge the historical specificity of the international state-system whose logic it explores; ignores the global capitalist economic context of inter-state conflict;

treats states as unified and homogeneous entities; and under-estimates the influence of ideological representations (as opposed to instrumental calculations) in motivating political action.[62]

For all that, Realism seems like a better error into which to fall than the fanciful belief that, thanks to political globalization, inter-state conflict is being transcended. Imperial power and geopolitical competition are fundamental features of the contemporary international system. To ignore this reality is to descend into apologetics, to seek to prettify world politics by ignoring the antagonisms that constitute it. The expression 'international community' does not refer to anything that actually exists: at best, it expresses an aspiration; at worst it mystifies the unequal and conflictual relationships on which all our fates depend.

The doctrine of humanitarian intervention – which asserts that sufficiently severe human rights violations justify over-riding state sovereignty – therefore needs to be treated with considerable scepticism. Great Powers have always asserted a right of intervention in the affairs of small countries. In the nineteenth century, they did so frankly invoking consider-ations of *Realpolitik*. Thus, in the era of the Holy Alliance after 1815, Castlereagh declared: 'The only safe principle is that of the Law of Nations – That no state has a right to endanger its neighbours by its internal Proceedings, and that if it does, provided they exercise a sound discretion, their right of Interference is clear.'[63] During the ideological con-frontation of the Cold War, intervention could be justified either to halt the spread of Communism (the Truman doc-trine) or to preserve the socialist system (the Brezhnev doctrine).

What principled justification could be given for overriding national sovereignty in the New World Order that took shape after 1989? The Carter administration in the late 1970s began to give prominence to the ideal that US policy was motivated by the defence of human rights around the world. The idea of specifically humanitarian intervention took shape during the terrible famines and wars that gripped

Africa in the 1980s and 1990s. NGOs such as Médecins sans Frontières asserted their right to supply relief to the victims of these crises irrespective of the wishes of the government of the country, and then backed this up by demanding Western military protection for their activities.[64]

After the end of the Cold War the idea of humanitarian intervention was generalized. A 1992 Carnegie Endowment Report called for 'a new principle of international relations: the destruction or displacement of groups of people within states can justify international intervention'.[65] The Bosnian War and the Rwandan genocide gave the doctrine greater credibility. Then came the Kosovo crisis, which seemed tailor-made as a means of establishing the new, revamped NATO as the vehicle for such interventions – though in this case the Western powers justified their military operations by a humanitarian catastrophe that would not have occurred in the absence of these operations.[66]

Scepticism is similarly in order concerning the increasing efforts to prosecute war crimes which Held, McGrew and their co-authors welcome as 'elements of cosmopolitan law'. As in the case of the 1999 Balkan War, what strikes one most is the selective nature of these prosecutions. What was probably the greatest war crime of the past generation – the devastation of Indochina by the United States – has gone completely unpunished; indeed, Henry Kissinger, one of its principal architects, continues to enjoy the material and moral rewards usually associated with the achievements of an honoured statesman.

The International Criminal Tribunal for the former Yugoslavia pursues war criminals under the authority of the UN Security Council, even though it is doubtful whether this body – dominated by the Great Powers – has the right under the Charter to create criminal jurisdictions, and is funded by private bodies like the Rockefeller Foundation and George Soros's Open Society Foundation.[67] Its decision in May 1999 to prosecute Milošević helped, with rather suspect good timing, to reinforce the pressures on him to seek a negotiated settlement of the Kosovo War, even though the greatest war crime for which he can be held responsible – the massacre at Srebrenica – had taken place almost four years earlier. Meanwhile, the US Congress has fiercely resisted attempts to create an International Criminal Court, properly constituted by treaty, because American troops might be held to account by it.

Far from transcending *Realpolitik*, contemporary humanitarian intervention is an instrument of it. As we have seen, this has not diminished the New Labour government's enthusiasm for Blair's 'Doctrine of the International Community'. In September 2000 the Labour and Liberal Democrat parties made a joint initiative calling for the UN to beef up its capacity for military intervention, and offering the expertise of the British military. The application of the doctrine has continued to be highly selective. Blair made a special trip to St Petersburg in March 2000, in advance of the Russian presidential elections, to express his support for Putin, and later welcomed Putin in London, despite the latter's brutal war in Chechenya. 'There is no doubt at all that he speaks our language on reform,' Blair declared.[68] One unstated criterion for intervention seems therefore to be whether or not the state committing human rights violations has nuclear weapons.

One reason for New Labour's support for humanitarian military operations may be the help these offer in addressing the now ancient problem of Britain's post-imperial role. Brzezinski brutally highlights how limited this role has become from Washington's perspective:

> Great Britain is not a geostrategic player. It has fewer major options [than France and Germany], it entertains no ambitious vision of Europe's future, and its relative decline has also reduced its capacity to play the traditional role of the European balancer. Its ambivalence regarding European unification and its waning special relationship with America have made Great Britain increasingly irrelevant in so far as the major choices confronting Europe's future are concerned. . . . It is America's key supporter, a very loyal ally, a vital military

base, and a close partner in critically important intelligence activities. Its friendship needs to be nourished, but its policies do not call for sustained attention.[69]

Britain has waged a series of colonial wars since 1945. Carrying these on in the name of human rights may help give its rulers a sense that they continue to bestride the globe. Continuing also to act as Washington's closest and most obedient European ally – bombing and blockading Iraq, for example, has become an Anglo-American policy – may strengthen this illusion. But an illusion it remains, and one made not better by becoming associated with the belief that the military might of the Great Powers can become an instrument of liberation. This belief ignores the interest that these states have in maintaining an international system riven with inequality and conflict. What, then, is to be done?

4

Alternatives

4.1 Bucking the market

The world at the beginning of the twenty-first century is dominated by a capitalism that is indeed more globally integrated than at any time of its history. It is also less regulated, more out control than it has been since the Great Depression of the 1930s. Contrary to what theorists of political globalization may claim, economic liberalization has not been counter-balanced by the development of genuinely multilateral forms of 'governance'. The state-system remains fundamentally anarchic, even if this may be obscured by the extent of American hegemony in the aftermath of the Cold War. Meanwhile inequality both on a global scale and within individual countries continues to grow, as successive studies and reports document with a regularity that might seem tedious if they did not serve as a reminder of the extent of socially caused suffering – what Pierre Bourdieu has called *La Misère du monde*, the weight of the world.

Supporters of the Third Way do not completely ignore these facts. A succession of crashes in 'emergent markets' –

Mexico 1994–5, East Asia 1997–8, Russia 1998 – has dramatized the extent to which individual countries have become vulnerable to sudden inflows and outflows of speculative investment, with devastating consequences for their economies.[1] Anthony Giddens acknowledges: 'The tendency of financial markets towards crisis is structural and needs to be coped with by collaborative intervention.' He calls for various measures to strengthen the international regulation of financial markets – the establishment of 'a world financial authority' to manage 'systemic risk in the world financial economy', the strengthening of the IMF as a step towards 'a global central bank' capable of acting as lender of last resort in financial crises, and 'the provision of orderly, official channels for the workout of debts'. He also proposes that the so-called Tobin Tax – the idea of taxing international financial speculation – 'should be properly examined and debated'.[2]

Giddens' position is representative of a widespread tendency that seeks to remedy the defects of economic neoliberalism through strengthening international institutions. Underlying this strategy is the thought that, while economic globalization may have undermined the powers of economic regulation of nation-states, multilateral bodies can impose new constraints on capital. Such is, for example, the stance taken by Jürgen Habermas in advocating what he calls 'a second, offensive variant of the Third Way':

> The perspective it offers turns on the notion that politics should take precedence over the logic of the market . . . the attempt to resolve the dilemma between disarming welfare-state democracy or rearming the nation-state leads us to look to larger political units and transnational systems that could compensate for the nation-state's functional losses in a way which need not snap the chain of democratic legitimation. The EU naturally comes to mind as an example of a democracy functioning beyond the limits of the nation-state. Of course, the creation of larger political entities does not by itself alter the process of competition between local production sites, that is, it does not challenge the primacy of market-

led integration per se. Politics will succeed in 'catching up' with globalized markets only if it eventually becomes possible to create an infrastructure capable of sustaining a global domestic politics without uncoupling it from democratic processes of legitimation.[3]

Social democrats hostile to the Third Way *tout court* have taken a similar stance. Using democratically accountable European institutions to control financial markets was one of the leitmotifs of Oskar Lafontaine's brief but exciting tenure as Finance Minister in Germany's Red–Green Coalition.[4] But the obdurate resistance that the unelected and independent European Central Bank put up to Lafontaine's campaign for lower interest rates – it carefully waited till after his resignation in March 1999 before cutting rates – should serve as a warning that international institutions do not necessarily promote greater democratic control, and indeed may work with rather than against markets.

Habermas shows some awareness of this. He notes that further European integration might not contribute towards the emergence of an authentic 'cosmopolitan democracy': 'if the federative project aimed only to field another global player with the clout of the United States, it would remain particularistic, merely endowing what asylum-seekers have come to know as "Fortress Europe" with a new – that is, an economic – dimension.'[5] But political integration, at either a regional or a genuinely global level, can equally well serve what Habermas calls 'particularistic' interests. He welcomed NATO's bombing campaign against Yugoslavia as furthering 'the idea of a human-rights [guided] domestication of the natural condition between states. The transformation of national law into cosmopolitan law thereby comes onto the agenda.'[6] In the light of the arguments of the last chapter, this position is, to say the least, naïve.

The leading international institutions as presently constituted – the G-7, the IMF, the World Bank, the WTO, NATO, the EU – operate in the interests of the United States and the other leading Western capitalist powers. Joseph

Stiglitz, former chairman of Bill Clinton's Council of Economic Advisers, wrote just ahead of a major anti-capitalist demonstration in Washington, DC, on 16 April 2000:

> Next week's meeting of the International Monetary Fund will bring to Washington, DC, many of the same demonstrators who trashed the World Trade Organization in Seattle last fall. They'll say the IMF is arrogant. They'll say the IMF doesn't really listen to the developing countries it is supposed to help. They'll say the IMF is secretive and insulated from democratic accountability. They'll say the IMF's economic 'remedies' often make things worse – turning slowdowns into recessions and recessions into depressions.
>
> And they'll have a point. I was chief economist at the World Bank until last November, during the gravest global economic crisis in a half-century. And I saw how the IMF, in tandem with the US Treasury Department, responded. And I was appalled.[7]

Stiglitz condemned the IMF and the US Treasury both for the secrecy with which they formulated policy and for the content of this policy itself – seeking to remedy financial crises caused at least in part by economic liberalization with budgetary austerity and yet more bouts of liberalization:

> Even internal critics, particularly those with direct democratic accountability, were kept in the dark. The Treasury Department is so arrogant about its economic analyses and prescriptions that it often keeps tight – much too tight – control over what even the president sees.
>
> Open discussion would have raised profound questions that still receive very little attention in the American press: To what extent did the IMF and the Treasury Department push policies that actually contributed to the increased global economic volatility? (Treasury pushed liberalization in Korea in 1993 over the opposition of the [President's] Council of Economic Advisers. Treasury won the internal White House battle, but Korea, and the world, paid a high price.) Were some of the IMF's harsh criticisms of East Asia intended to detract attention from the agency's own culpability? Most

importantly, did America – and the IMF – push policies because we, or they, believed the policies would help East Asia or because we believed they would benefit financial interests in the United States and the advanced industrial world? And if we believed our policies were helping East Asia, where was the evidence? As a participant in these debates, I got to see this evidence. There was none.[8]

Given this performance by the IMF, its further strengthening – proposed by Giddens – hardly seems a very attractive idea. It should not, moreover, be forgotten that these policies were carried out by US Treasury Secretary Robert Rubin and his deputy and successor Lawrence Summers while a champion of the Third Way occupied the White House. Stiglitz's criticisms were part of a broader assault on the Washington consensus mounted by orthodox economists – Paul Krugman and Jeffrey Sachs were two other examples of this trend. In the wake of the East Asian and Russian crashes, there was much talk in Western capitals of developing what came to be known as a 'new financial architecture' for the world economy. Tony Blair set out a representative set of proposals in a keynote speech:

The fact is that the Bretton Woods machinery was set up for the post-war world. The world has moved on. And we need to modernize the international financial architecture to make it appropriate for the new world. The lesson of the Asian crisis is that it is better to invest in countries where you have openness, independent central banks, properly functioning financial systems and independent courts, where you do not have to bribe or rely on favours from those in power.

We have therefore proposed that we should make greater transparency the keystone of reform. Transparency about individual countries' economic policies through adherence to new codes of conduct on monetary and fiscal policy; about individual countries' financial positions through new internationally agreed accounting standards and a new code of corporate governance; and new openness too about IMF and World Bank discussions and policies.[9]

This represents a much less radical, and more superficial, diagnosis of the failings of financial markets than that offered by Giddens. Thus the latter writes:

> The common thread in all of these [financial crises during the 1980s and 1990s] was the volatile nature of capital flows. What happened resembled financial panics of earlier times, but took place with greater speed, scope and intensity because of the instantaneous character of global market reactions today. It isn't only that there can be a sudden surge of capital out of a country or area – capital can rush into favoured hot spots as well. Both processes have undesirable effects. The damage produced by rapid outflows of money has been evident in each successive crisis. But surges of capital inwards can also have destabilizing effects, leading to the over-valuation of exchange-rates, rising property and asset prices, and a bubble economy.[10]

This analysis is at least tacitly critical of neo-liberalism, since financial deregulation has greatly facilitated international capital mobility. For Blair, by contrast, the Asian crisis was largely the fault of the affected countries themselves for lacking the appropriate levels of financial 'transparency'. Assertions of this kind imply the kind of view widely prevalent in the US that the upheavals of 1997–8 were caused by East Asian 'crony capitalism', with its intimate and secretive connections between bureaucrats, bankers and industrialists. The remedy is implicit in the diagnosis: Japan, South Korea and the rest should adopt Western – or more specifically Anglo-American – financial structures involving independent central banks, 'prudent' monetary and fiscal policies, deregulated markets, and the like. Far then from neo-liberalism being the disease to which East Asia and Russia succumbed, it represents, according to Blair, the cure for their ills.

Such an assessment has the advantage – or disadvantage – of letting the Western capitalist countries off the hook. Is the US or Britain innocent of intimate links between politicians and business? 'Western crony capitalism' was how the veteran financial journalist John Plender described the rescue mounted in October 1998 by the Federal Reserve Board and fifteen major American and European investment banks after the hedge fund Long-Term Capital Management (LTCM) had been bankrupted by the Russian financial crash. LTCM's staff included a former vice-chairman of the Fed; its elaborate web of speculation had been spun on behalf of, among others, various leading investment bankers involved in the rescue.[11]

There are, of course, other much more routine connections between the state and capital in the Western liberal democracies. The business executives who poured tens of millions of dollars into Bill Clinton's re-election campaign in 1996 and into Al Gore's campaign in 2000 did not do so out of pure altruism or in the hope of spending a night in the Lincoln bedroom, but in the expectation of favourable treatment by the administration. George W. Bush's corporate backers lashed out even more to win control of the White House: spending by political parties and their supporters in the US elections of 2000 is estimated to have totalled a record $3 billion.[12] Ronald Dworkin comments: 'Our politics are a disgrace, and money is at the root of the problem.'[13] Blair has not concealed his admiration for the American political system: he has, for example, sought to weaken Labour's links with the trade unions by raising election funding from wealthy entrepreneurs. His policy of stuffing government bodies with business figures is not simply a quid pro quo: it reflects his sincere belief that the public sector is best run by private enterprise. But it is hard to see, from a democratic point of view, how these arrangements are, in principle, any different from those he and other Western leaders condemned in East Asia.

Finally, Blair's diagnosis ignores the role of Western financial markets in engineering the 'emergent market' crises of the 1990s. In each case these involved, as Giddens says, destabilizing surges of speculative investment from the advanced economies into favoured countries, followed, when conditions changed, by even more destructive outflows of capital. After the Mexican crash, a Wall Street money manager cheerfully explained the casual way in which these decisions are made: 'We went into Latin America not knowing anything about the place. Now we are leaving without knowing anything about it.'[14] Yet interventions by the G-7 and the IMF after each of these crises were intended to rescue not the affected country but the speculators by ensuring their loans were repaid. This alarmed even many neoliberal commentators concerned by the resulting growth in 'moral hazard': in other words, the rescues would encourage the speculators to make even more risky investments in the future, confident that they would not have to pay for any mistakes they made.

Keynes famously compared the financial markets to a casino: 'Speculators may do no harm as bubbles on a steady stream of enterprise. But the position is serious when enterprise becomes the bubble of a whirlwind of speculation. When the capital development of a country becomes the by-product of a casino, the job is likely to be ill-done.'[15] But even he didn't imagine a casino where the bank indemnifies the gamblers whenever their bets go wrong.

Blair's view of the 'new financial architecture' – that it should remain essentially the same as the old, while continuing to press national governments to adopt neo-liberal policies – is indicative of the general direction of Western policy under Third Way leadership.[16] Developments at the World Bank are symptomatic. The World Bank is generally regarded as the softer, more accommodating partner of the IMF, though its responsibility for making loans to Third World countries has given it a key role in imposing the Washington consensus.

In November 1999 Stiglitz announced he was resigning as the Bank's chief economist before his three-year contract had expired. His public pronouncements, for example supporting Malaysia's adoption of capital controls in 1998 and attacking Russia's flagrantly corrupt privatization, had become increasingly irritating for the American Treasury. The *Financial Times* reported: 'It had been rumoured for weeks that

Larry Summers, Treasury secretary, had made the reappointment of World Bank president James Wolfensohn for five more years at the bank conditional upon Mr Stiglitz's departure.'[17]

The clear-out at the World Bank continued the following summer. Ravi Kanbur, author of its annual *World Development Report*, resigned from the Bank in June 2000. His draft had been changed to play down the role of 'empowerment' – a code-word for redistribution – in reducing poverty and to emphasize instead the importance of 'opportunity', in other words, economic liberalization and growth. According to the *Financial Times*, 'many saw the resignation as an important victory for orthodox free-trade and growth-based solutions within the economics profession'. Tim Geithner, Assistant US Treasury Secretary for International Affairs, told the paper: 'There is no serious challenge to the proposition that growth is central to development.'[18]

It is certainly true that no serious challenge to this proposition comes from Third Way quarters. Bill Clinton told the 2000 World Economic Forum at Davos: 'I think we have to re-affirm unambiguously that open markets and rules-based trade are the best engine we know of to lift living standards, reduce environmental destruction and build shared prosperity.'[19] During the protests at Seattle, Clare Short, British Secretary of State for International Development and one of the few representatives of Old Labour in the Blair government, called the WTO 'a precious international institution' and said that 'those who make blanket criticisms of the WTO are working against, not for, the interests of the poor and the powerless.'[20]

The intellectual case behind pronouncements such as Clinton's and Short's has been made most powerfully by *Financial Times* columnist Martin Wolf. Attacking Kanbur and his supporters, he wrote:

The governments of the world's poorest countries *must* 'go for growth above all else'. It is no accident that east Asia saw the biggest reductions in the number of people on incomes

below a dollar a head (at PPP [purchasing power parity])
between 1988 and 1997. . . . That, after all, was the region
with the fastest growth,. . . . Growth means more goods and
services, greater choice and more resources for governments.
Discussions of poverty alleviation that do not lay primary
emphasis on growth are, therefore, 'like Hamlet without the
prince', as Larry Summers, US Treasury secretary, has said.[21]

But Wolf's claim that trade-based economic growth reduces
global inequality has come under challenge, notably from
the economists Matthias Lundberg and Branko Milanovic.
They distinguish between three concepts of inequality –
inequality within countries, reflected in, for example, income
disparities; international inequality, that is, the differences in
countries' average per capita incomes; and global inequality,
which combines these two concepts, referring to income
differentials between all individuals in the world.

Lundberg and Milanovic point out that Wolf has relied on
studies measuring changes in *international* inequality. But
'an international inequality measure hardly gauges the real
extent of global income disparity, for it assumes that every
Chinese, and every American has the same national mean
income.' By contrast, the world Gini coefficient, which seeks
to estimate global inequality by combining domestic and
international inequality measures, rose from 63 in 1988 to
66 in 1993. Other research in which Lundberg and Milanovic are involved finds that,

in the short term, greater openness in trade slows income
growth among the poorest 40 per cent of the population.
Although over the longer term everybody benefits from trade
openness, the costs of adjustment are borne exclusively by the
poor.
    The poor are far more vulnerable to shifts in relative
international prices. And countries' openness to trade is
clearly exacerbating this vulnerability.[22]

Despite their acceptance of core neo-liberal tenets, Third
Way governments deny that they have condemned the

world's poor to rely on what Ronald Reagan called 'the magic of the marketplace' to improve their plight. Gordon Brown and Clare Short sought strenuously to associate New Labour with the initiative taken in June 1999 by the G-8 (the G-7 plus Russia) to offer 'enhanced' debt relief to the poorest countries. The scale of the debt repayments being made by the most impoverished Third World states to Western banks was causing widespread outrage in the rich countries themselves, helping to stimulate the development of mass movements such as Jubilee 2000. G-7 governments were under increasing pressure to act. But debt relief was targeted at a limited number of countries – the so-called 'heavily indebted poor countries' (HIPCs) – and made conditional on implementation of the usual IMF/World Bank package of neo-liberal measures. These tough terms, combined with the reluctance of the US Congress to release its share of the funds, meant that not one single country had benefited from debt relief by the time the next G-8 summit took place in July 2000. Moreover, Oxfam calculated that, even if implemented, 'enhanced' HIPC relief would still leave five out of twelve of the poorest countries still repaying more to their Western creditors than their combined health and education budgets.[23] 'The debt relief initiative is becoming one of the scandals of the twenty-first century,' said Zie Arlyo of Uganda Debt Network. 'Debt relief is a hoax.'[24]

The claims made on behalf of Third Way governments that they represent new ways of regulating capitalism have thus proved false. They have in fact embraced and in certain respects radicalized the neo-liberal policies of their predecessors. The Blair government is, for example, transferring the management of state schools and the provision of other educational services to private companies. Meanwhile, in the European arena, Britain under New Labour presses for the adoption by the EU of more 'flexible' labour-market policies.

But this is by no means an exclusively British phenomenon. The Schröder government, though much more constrained by an assertive labour movement, is pushing in the same direction. The *Financial Times* greeted its decision in

December 1999 to abolish capital gains tax on German companies' selling their holdings in other companies with the headlines 'Christmas Comes Early for German Board-rooms' and 'Investment Bankers Eye New Pickings'. According to the paper, the decision 'frees up corporate Germany to indulge in a wave of mergers and acquisitions'. One analyst said: 'This means a lot more business for M&A people. They'll be knocking on doors they haven't been knocking on before'.[25] Where its conservative–liberal prede-cessor had failed, the Red–Green coalition was able to undertake this major move towards a more Anglo-American model of capitalism committed to maximizing 'shareholder value' – i.e. short-term profits.

Manuel Castells offers a charitable interpretation of this process:

> The ironic twist of political history is that the reformers who enacted globalization, all over the world, came mostly from the left, breaking with their past as supporters of government control of the economy. It would be a mistake to consider this a proof of political opportunism. It was, rather, realism about new economic and technological developments, and a sense of the quickest way to take economies out of their relative stagnation.[26]

But the opposition between realism and opportunism that Castells relies on here is not helpful. For one thing it misses out the principled commitment to liberal capitalism charac-teristic certainly of key New Labour figures such as Tony Blair and Peter Mandelson. Their courtship of the business world and enthusiasm for the privatization of public services has reflected no mere expediency but the sincere, indeed dogmatic, belief that private entrepreneurs just are better at running things than anyone else, even when empirical evi-dence – for example, the fiascos of the Millennium Dome, Wheel and Bridge built along the Thames to celebrate the year 2000, let alone the much greater catastrophe of rail privatization – suggested the contrary.

For another thing, Castells' appeal to realism suppresses the availability of alternatives to neo-liberalism. For example, Malaysia was able to weather the Asian crisis relatively easily thanks to the imposition of capital controls restricting the speculative movement of money in and out of the country. Prime Minister Mahathir Mohamed presides over a demagogic authoritarian regime but even economic commentators sympathetic to neo-liberal orthodoxy had to concede that he had successfully bucked the market. There are other measures that could be tried to control markets, for example the Tobin Tax on financial speculation. Rather surprisingly, Giddens points to the reason why it has not been taken up: 'The main barrier ... does not concern problems of evasion, or implementation more generally, but – so far – lack of political will.'[27] But nowhere has political will been more lacking than in the US and British Treasuries, and in the White House and 10 Downing Street, despite Giddens' entrée to these last two establishments at least. Those who seek alternatives to neo-liberalism must look elsewhere than the Third Way.

4.2   Nine anti-capitalist theses

Perry Anderson is right: 'the Third Way is the best ideological shell of neo-liberalism today.'[28] This does not mean that neo-liberalism could not, and will not, find other shells, but currently the idea that efficiency as the market defines it and justice as socialists have conceived it can be reconciled is the most politically influential ideology both in the advanced capitalist countries and in the leading Third World states.

It does not, however, go unchallenged. The Seattle demonstrations at the end of November 1999 marked the beginning of a wave of anti-capitalist protests. The experience of neo-liberal policies provided the impetus for this movement; at the same time, the enhanced role of various international institutions as vehicles for the leading capitalist states to hammer out their policies offered highly visible targets for pressure and protest. In the year 2000 the leading venues of these demonstrations were Washington, Millau, Melbourne, Prague, Seoul and Nice. No doubt there will be many others in the years ahead. Defenders of the Third Way have been quick to dismiss the anti-capitalist movement. Thus John Lloyd, who has divided his time over the past decade between apologias for New Labour and the quixotic attempt to persuade Western opinion-formers that first Boris Yeltsin and then (even less plausibly) Vladimir Putin were Russia's only hope of a prosperous and democratic future, patronizingly dismissed the French peasant leader José Bové as representing a regressive, confused, nationalist movement:

> Mr Bové, amiable, moustachioe'd, media friendly, unites too much under his banner to be coherent. His movement runs on the internet and the cellphone yet vilifies the science and the multinationals that created them. It seeks alliances with groups whose members are largely the beneficiaries – as citizens of the rich, powerful and globally competitive French economy – of globalization. But he has struck a chord. . . . It is the chord of an alternative civilization, France; and an alternative lifestyle, simplicity. Neither is fully possible in the real world: but in the media-led, festive world created around the peasants' protests, they seem to be.[29]

The anti-capitalist movement is indeed still in many ways incohate and incoherent. But it is clear about what it is against: as the slogan popularized by Bové himself has it, '*Le Monde N'est Pas Une Marchandise*' – The World Is Not For Sale. In other words, the protests are directed against the relentless commodification of everything – down to the genes that are the very stuff of life itself – that the neo-liberal hegemony has promoted and Third Way governments simply reinforced. It is merely a silly slur to accuse the protesters of nostalgic nationalism: they have been characterized rather by their internationalism – Bové was among the numerous activists from all over the world who took part in the Seattle demonstrations. To this extent the theorists of political globalization are right: even the very limited forms of multilateralism that have developed in the past generation have helped to promote the emergence of what David Held, Anthony McGrew and their co-authors call 'transnational social movements'. Now these movements are beginning to find a common focus and to throw up intellectual spokespeople in the shape of figures such as Pierre Bourdieu, Susan George and George Monbiot.[30] A powerful critique of neo-liberalism, and alternative ideology to the Third Way, is emerging. How better therefore to conclude this book than by setting out some theses that seem to me crucial elements of such an ideology?

Thesis 1 *The enemy is not globalization, but global capitalism.*

Lloyd is typical of neo-liberals and defenders of the Third Way (including some who ought to know better) in accusing anti-capitalists of opposing globalization *tout court*. In fact, anti-capitalists do not oppose growing connections between people in different countries. If anything it is Western governments – currently dominated by the centre-left – who are seeking to impede these connections by capitulating and in some cases encouraging racist media campaigns against asylum seekers and 'economic migrants'. But, as I have tried to show in the preceding chapters, the predominant form of globalization is economic, and takes the form of the integration of the world economy on the basis of the dominance of large-scale capitalist industrial and financial institutions. Crediting these institutions with the scientific and technical innovations of the past generation is a flagrant example of what Marx called 'commodity fetishism'.

Thesis 2 *The core institutions of global capitalism are the multinational corporations, the leading capitalist states and the international institutions that reflect their interests.*

'The operations of MNCs are central to processes of economic globalization,' Held, McGrew and their collaborators write.[31] In 1998 there were 53,000 multinational corporations with 450,000 foreign subsidiaries and global sales of $9.5 trillion. They account for two-thirds of world trade; one-third is taken up with transactions between subsidiaries of the same company.

Figures for foreign direct investment understate the extent of
the MNCs' economic power: thus about a fifth of world gross
fixed capital formation is undertaken by the foreign affiliates of
multinational corporations. Moreover, these companies are
involved in global production networks linking them to other,
usually much smaller, firms.[32]

The MNCs are still largely based in the advanced capitalist
countries where the bulk of their investments are concentrated.[33] They have enormous influence over the governments
of these countries, which, for example, compete to offer favourable packages designed to attract new inward investments. The
same process of bargaining and influence is now developing at
the international level. Thus the prospect of further trade liberalization, particularly with respect to services, at the WTO
summit in Seattle helped to spawn various lobbying alliances of
MNCs – for example, the US Coalition of Service Industries,
the European Service Leaders' Group, Accelerated Tariff Liberalization.[34] Other groups – for example the influential Transatlantic Business Dialogue composed of about a hundred
American and European chief executives – are pressing for more
comprehensive changes that will give the MNCs unhindered
access to every national economy.[35]

The growing power of the big corporations is alarming even
some of a strongly pro-capitalist persuasion, for example the
Wall Street investment consultant Henry Kaufman: 'What, then
is the longer-term challenge to the US's imperfect democracy?
The chief threat lies with the current fashion for merger and
concentration, which has taken hold not merely in the financial
sector but also in car manufacturing, telecommunications, air-
line manufacturing, petroleum, broadcasting, computers and
software.' Kaufman is concerned about the negative impact of
this process on competition and thereby on economic efficiency:
'Although the established dominant company or companies
may be vulnerable on the product or service side, their enormous capital advantage allows them simply to acquire innovations, or copy them, thereby outlasting their smaller rivals
during the competitive phase.'[36]

The process of economic concentration and centralization
also has political implications. This is not to say that international institutions such as the IMF and WTO are simply tools
of the MNCs, any more than nation-states are. Nevertheless

these institutions largely serve as arenas in which the advanced capitalist states, and the economic interests associated with them, can arbitrate and regulate their conflicts on terms that are relatively favourable to the largest power of all, the United States. The idea that the international institutions represent the embryonic form of 'global governance' is, alas, a dream.

Thesis 3 *Capital is a relation, not a thing.*

There is, however, a tendency among anti-capitalists to conceive global capitalism as a malign conspiracy. This is personified in the multinationals, which are often portrayed, rather like the Borg in *Star Trek*, as a vast alien entity, constantly on the move, seeking to assimilate and to destroy. But capitalism is not reducible to its institutional forms, including the MNCs. As Marx was the first to point out, capital is a relation, not a thing. It is an impersonal structure of competitive accumulation which none can control, even the largest individual capitals.[37]

This abstract theoretical proposition has important concrete implications. It is clear that central to contemporary economic globalization is the development of more internationally integrated financial markets. But financial markets are not specific institutions, though they have important institutional presuppositions – thus their greater integration over the past generation has been greatly facilitated by the policies of deregulation pursued by leading Western capitalist governments. Financial markets are a cluster of relationships linking together a variety of actors – investment banks, hedge funds, private speculators, central banks, and the like – caught up in processes from which they seek to wrest the maximum advantage, but which dominate them.

Thesis 4 *The requirements of capitalist reproduction set limits to its regulation and reform.*

Capitalism thus conceived has certain conditions of reproduction. These set limits to the extent to which its structures can be reformed or regulated. It is these limits, in turn, that explain the difficulties that social-democratic governments have faced in the past in seeking to humanize and democratize capitalism. Policies that are perceived to threaten the conditions of stable and profitable capitalist production evoke a response – most notably capital flight – that undermines the offending government and, typically, compels it to abandon the policies in question. It is important to see that this process requires no conspiracy on the part of the capitalists themselves. The beauty of capital flight from this perspective is that this mechanism requires no concerted resolve to force a change in government policy. All that is needed for it to operate is a mass of self-seeking decisions by individual investors that the offending policy makes it rational for them to move their capital elsewhere, with the cumulative effect – usually in the form of a currency crisis – of bringing about a policy-reversal.[38]

This analysis does not imply that it is futile to seek reforms. One of the main reproaches against the Third Way is that its policies operate well within the limits set by the requirements of capitalist reproduction. A decent minimum wage, more generous pensions and efficient public transport would not, for example, bring British capitalism tumbling down, yet New Labour shuns them. There are specific reforms demanded by the pressing issues of the day – thus the Tobin Tax has been taken up in France by the campaigning movement ATTAC and the influential left-wing monthly *Le Monde diplomatique*. Mobilizing support for this kind of measure could achieve a redistribution of wealth from rich to poor; it would also test where the limits of reform actually lie. But an effective anti-capitalist movement must be aware that these limits exist.

Thesis 5 *The capital-relation implies the dependence of capital on its opposite, wage-labour.*

Capitalism is not simply a structured relationship among capitals. Despite their differences and conflicts, the latter share a common dependence on the wage-labour from whose exploitation, directly or indirectly, their profits derive. This is, of course, the central proposition of Marx's theory of the capitalist mode of production: capital is constituted by its contradictory relationship with wage-labour.

It is not a currently fashionable idea. Castells, for example, dismisses the widely held belief that globalization is ushering in 'the end of work': 'the number of paid jobs in the world . . . is at its highest peak in human history and going up. And rates of participation by the adult population are increasing everywhere because of the unprecedented incorporation of women into the labour market. To ignore these elementary data is to ignore our society.' He insists accordingly that, 'in modern societies, *paid working time* structures social time'.[39] But Castells also argues – along with many other social theorists – that this extension of the wage-relation is accompanied by a fragmentation and individualization of work that has radically weakened organized labour.

But the situation is much less clear-cut than this argument might suggest. Certainly capitalist restructuring since the late 1970s – and the defeated struggles that were necessary to overcome resistance to this process – have undermined trade-union power right across the advanced capitalist countries. Furthermore, the intensity of international competition means that the impulse to restructure is now permanent, placing workforces under constant pressure. None of this means, however, that collective working-class organization and action are obsolete, for three reasons among others.

First, the very intensity of pressures in the workplace, and the pervasive job insecurity that is a consequence of economic liberalization, can generate resistance. This may help to explain the extent of the French public-sector strikes of November–December 1995 and the popular support they received. Secondly, despite all their efforts to out-source, contract out and atomize their workforces, multinational corporations remain vulnerable to strategically placed groups of workers. The United States – where the weakening of organized labour has gone furthest in the advanced economies – saw in the late 1990s a number of big companies hit by successful strikes.

Thirdly, some of the changes associated with the 'New Economy' have actually increased corporate vulnerability. The extremely rapid impact of the fuel blockades mounted in France, Britain and other European countries in September 2000, even though they were carried out in the main by coalitions of small employers rather than by trade unionists, demonstrated how rapidly contemporary capitalist economies, reliant on just-in-time techniques that are designed to keep stocks and therefore costs low, can topple over once the flow of deliveries is interrupted.

Thesis 6 *The relationship between organized labour and other social movements is in process of being redefined.*

For the past generation much ink has been spilt over the nature of what are called (now rather inaccurately since they are getting on a bit) the 'new social movements' concerned with issues such as the liberation of women, blacks, lesbians and gays and the destruction of the environment. Typically they have been conceived of as challenging and perhaps displacing the traditional labour movement – partly because of the perceived 'economism' of trade unions and social-democratic parties preoccupied with bread-and-butter issues, partly because the new movements were thought to be contesting forms of domination irreducible to capitalist exploitation and the patterns of class conflict it generated. Giddens' earlier theoretical work was intended at least in part to articulate the kind of critique of Marxism required by the new forms of politics – 'life politics', as he put it.[40]

This kind of counterposition of organized labour and other social movements is now evidently inadequate. This is because those engaged in different kinds of collective action are increasingly motivated by a sense that, beyond their specific concerns or grievances, lies a common enemy – global capitalism. The significance of the Seattle protests was not simply that they helped to precipitate the collapse of the WTO summit, but that they brought together core elements of American labour – Teamsters, machinists, longshoremen, auto-workers – with activists concerned with issues such as environmental destruction and Third World debt: 'Teamsters and Turtles – Together At Last!' as one slogan had it.

This convergence represented a potentially crucial move towards a process in which both parties began to redefine their conceptions of their own and each other's motives and interests. Trade unionists in the North might thus start to see workers in the South less as competitors undercutting their own wages and conditions but rather as their counterparts facing a much starker and more brutal version of the exploitation they themselves suffered. Environmental and Third World activists might similarly begin to perceive organized labour not as a conservative, even reactionary, force inclined towards protectionist and nationalist policies, but as a potential ally with the collective economic strength needed decisively to challenge the institutions of capitalist power.

This process of mutual redefinition is fragile and eminently reversible. Both parties are liable to their own version of the danger that constantly faces reform movements – incorporation in the institutions from which they are demanding change. Trade-union leaders in both the US and Britain have, on the whole, been extremely unwilling to do anything that might seriously undermine their relationships with, respectively, the Clinton–Gore administration and New Labour, even though they have received in exchange the most petty concessions. Non-governmental organizations can also find themselves reduced to the status of useful idiots of the powerful. The fact that Bernard Kouchner, founder of Médecins sans Frontières, now presides as NATO's proconsul in Kosovo is an apt symbol of this danger. But there is nothing inevitable about such an outcome.

Thesis 7 *Defending the environment means challenging capitalism.*

This convergence reflects more than just a passing mood. The structural realities supporting it are most evident in the case of the environment. Freeing capitalism from the constraints to which it was subject a generation ago has contributed materially to the progressive, and increasingly catastrophic, destruction of the natural environment on which all life on the planet depends. Centre-left politicians proclaim their commitment to halting and reversing this process, but show no sign of a willingness to adopt the radical measures that would be required to make these declarations more than effusions of good intentions. In the first instance this reflects the fact that Western electorates are embedded in habits – above all, reliance on the privately owned motor car – damaging to the environment.

More fundamentally, however, Third Way politicians are unwilling to confront the structures of capitalist power that underpin these patterns of individual behaviour. The Clinton administration headed up the campaign by American multinationals to block proposals at successive UN conferences for the imposition of tight targets on countries to reduce polluting emissions. The Blair government, having unexpectedly reached the targets set for it at the 1997 Kyoto conference ahead of time thanks to the replacement of coal by natural gas in British power stations, plans to sell the amount undershot as 'carbon credits' – rights to pollute – to the US under the system proposed at Kyoto of emissions trading (itself both a sign of how market priorities are allowed to penetrate and to pervert every aspect of life and a mechanism that will allow the American economy to carry on pumping out 24 per cent of all greenhouse gases).[41] Both governments pressed for the introduction into Europe of genetically modified organisms, despite the enormous potential hazard to the environment that these represent.

It is hard to see how the measures required to save the environment can be made consistent with the requirements of capitalist reproduction. At the national level, phasing out the private automobile, or at least drastically reducing its use, would require, on the one hand, large-scale investment in public transport that would bust the spending targets required by neo-liberal economic policies and more generally raise the profile and prestige of the public sector in policy-making and political debate, and, on the other, confronting the constellation of capitalist interests bound up with the status quo, above all the fossil fuel corporations – the oil companies, car manufacturers, and the like. The steps required internationally to reverse the greenhouse effect – monitoring the reduction of polluting emissions, reforestation, promoting alternative forms of transport and energy supply, etc. – would entail some sort of system of collectively agreed resource-allocation that it would be tempting to call planning had this not become an idea whose time, all are apparently agreed, has definitively gone. 'Life politics' today can only be anti-capitalist politics.[42]

Thesis 8   *Alternative models of society will emerge from the anti-capitalist movements.*

Socialist planning was, of course, discredited by the collapse of the bureaucratic command economies of the Soviet Union and the other Stalinist states. This failure provides defenders of neo-liberalism with their standard response to anti-capitalists – the demand that they explain what their alternative would be. As we saw in the Introduction, what Giddens described as 'the death of socialism' – by which he meant the death of what I called economic statism, that is, an economic system steered by the nation-state – provides the Third Way with its starting point.

At one level, the demand that anti-capitalist critics specify their alternative to capitalism is a perfectly legitimate request that no one could reasonably reject. But the discourse in which this question has tacitly figured since the collapse of 'existing socialism' has been one that serves, in effect, to close down the debate about alternatives. Implicitly the choice presented is that between neo-liberalism and economic statism (usually in its Stalinist version). Not simply does this suppress the whole range of other possibilities extending between, and indeed beyond, these two options, but the disintegration of one purported variant of socialism is held to discredit all the others – reformist, revolutionary, utopian and anarchist – even though they are united in their quarrelsome diversity chiefly by hostility to Stalinism.

The emergence of the anti-capitalist movement provides an opportunity to end this stultified debate. The very incoherence of the movement – that is, the presence within it of a variety of ideological currents, Green, socialist, Third Worldist, anarchist – that are themselves internally complex is likely to encourage the elaboration of different, mutually incompatible alternative models. Through attempts theoretically to articulate and prac- tically to implement these models we are likely to develop a much clearer sense of how we can transcend capitalism.

Thesis 9   *Transcending capitalism requires a revolutionary transformation of society.*

Even granted the argument of Thesis 8, there is an ambiguity in the current stance of the anti-capitalist movement that must be confronted. Naturally criticism is focused on one particular variant of capitalism – the Anglo-American model that neo- liberalism is trying to generalize. This leaves open the question of whether the alternative should be another, more humane and democratic form of capitalism – for example, what is sometimes called the Rhineland model of regulated capitalism associated with continental Europe and Japan – or whether we should seek to replace capitalism altogether. Some of those critical of the Third Way, for example Bourdieu and Lafontaine, seem to advocate an international version of Rhineland capitalism, in which the European Union provides the regulation that the nation-state can no longer supply. In part for reasons touched on in §4.1 above, this does not seem to me a realistic strategy.[43]

In my view the problem lies deeper than the particular version of capitalism that currently confronts us. It is inherent in the logic of capital accumulation to treat both human beings and the planet itself as mere raw materials to be used and, if necessary, destroyed. The systematic removal over the past twenty years of the restraints that were imposed on capitalism in the mid-twentieth century has brought this into sharp relief. What is needed is a break with the very logic of capital, and its replacement by a different one – one that, at the minimum, gives priority to human needs and subjects the allocation of resources to democratic control. Traditionally a society meeting these conditions has been called 'socialism'. Whatever may be required to gain admittance to the White House, I see nothing wrong in continuing to use this word and seeking to achieve the society that it names.

Bringing such a society into existence will be an arduous task. It will mean a revolution – in other words, a systemic transformation of society, the replacement of one social logic with another. The idea of the Third Way is attractive to those who believe that such an upheaval is not feasible, and indeed is undesirable and unnecessary. But, as we have seen, the Third Way is but an ideological façade behind which capitalism continues on its brutal and destructive way. Addressing the real ills of the world as currently constituted means taking a path that, having been abandoned by most, has fallen into neglect. But it is, I believe, the only way through which we can hope to avoid repeating in the twenty-first century some new version of the horrors that made the twentieth century so terrible a nightmare.

Afterword

The attraction of the idea of the Third Way lies in the promise it offers of escaping the dead-ends we have inherited from the past. Confronted with the unpalatable alternatives of Stalinism and Thatcherism, who wouldn't prefer a third way? To this promise of liberation is added the sense – deriving from the collapse of the Eastern bloc and the impact of economic globalization – of living in a new era. The resulting cocktail helps to explain why many who are rightly sceptical about the actually existing Third Way nevertheless hanker after some other, more plausible version of the same formula that lies somewhere awaiting discovery.[1]

The upshot of this book is, to begin with, that the Third Way that is now on offer does not constitute an attractive option for the left. Far from breaking with the neo-liberal policies of the New Right, it has continued and, in certain ways, radicalized them. The Blair government has carried privatization further than its Tory predecessors dared. It does not follow that no more beneficent measures have been passed, but the balance is greatly outweighed by those that further entrench market relations in every corner of social life. In both the United States and Britain the cruelty of

Third Way social policy has been masked by the effects of the economic boom of the 1990s – without the very rapid fall in American unemployment during the second half of the last decade, the impact of welfare 'reform' in particular would have been truly appalling. But the victims of a future recession will find themselves far more exposed to the full rigours of the market than those who lost their jobs under Reagan and Thatcher.

A second major theme of this book has been to stress the continuities in both the world economy and global politics. It is no part of my argument to deny that a far greater degree of global economic integration exists than did a generation ago; similarly, only a fool would refuse to recognize that the international political order has experienced profound changes as a result of the end of the Cold War and the collapse of the Soviet Union. Nevertheless, it is important to understand the limits of the changes that have taken place. In particular, the claims made for the 'New Economy' are vastly exaggerated. Capitalism has not, thanks to the IT revolution, transcended the cycle of boom and slump: indeed the febrile, speculative character of the American expansion since the early 1990s suggests that, if anything, we are entering an era of greater economic instability. International politics meanwhile displays contradictory tendencies: on the one hand, the higher profile of the leading international institutions reflects a US strategy designed to mobilize the resources of, and regulate the conflicts within, the Western bloc under American leadership; on the other hand, the removal of the straitjacket imposed by the Cold War has introduced a fluid situation in which the manoeuvres of the Great Powers are becoming much more complex and unpredictable. Underlying both these tendencies is a world system that continues to be riven by inter-state tensions. John Rawls' 'Law of the Peoples', like Immanuel Kant's 'Perpetual Peace', is a long way from being realized.

Where stands the left in this world that is still governed by the logic of capital accumulation? Behind the experience of the Third Way lie the protracted efforts of the labour movement over the past century to reform capitalism. Far from renewing social democracy, the Third Way amounts to an attempt to mobilize the political capital of the reformist left in support of a project that abandons substantial reforms altogether and instead embraces neo-liberalism. It does not follow that reformism of a more traditional kind is therefore dead. As I have already noted, Bourdieu, Habermas and Lafontaine have all sought, in effect, to rehabilitate social democracy by transposing it to the European arena.

A revived reformism would, however, have to confront a significantly different context from that in which social democracy originally flourished. The problem of agency is especially acute. Traditionally social democracy saw the nation-state as both the framework and the means of achieving change. Economic globalization has not eliminated the power of the nation-state, but the latter's room for manoeuvre is undoubtedly more confined that it was in the era of economic autarky in the mid-twentieth century. At the same time, the drive to impose neo-liberal policies globally, combined with the quantum leap in the facility of communication that is one of the real effects of the IT revolution, has promoted the development of international movements of resistance. This implies the formation of a political arena broader even than the European Union.

In an effort to clarify the meaning of anti-capitalism, I set out in §4.2 above nine theses. There is no reason in principle why someone committed to a reformist approach could not accept most or even all of them. During the 1930s Labour left-wingers such as Stafford Cripps envisaged an elected government using constitutional means to force through a programme of socialist reforms over capitalist opposition.[2] A variant of this strategy could be adapted to seek a series of structural reforms whose cumulative effect would be radically to transform global capitalism.[3] Beyond broader strategic considerations, demands for specific reformist measures are far from having lost their political resonance: thus opinion polls consistently show strong public support for the renationalization of Britain's railways.

One dimension along which a genuine renewal of the left would develop would be an exploration of the scope for a robust form of social democracy in the era of global capitalism. In certain respects this process has already begun, although it does not use the language of traditional socialism. As I noted in the last chapter, the NGOs that have been central to the international campaigns against Third World debt and the WTO are increasingly confronted with traditional reformist dilemmas: Should they seek the reform or the abolition of the international capitalist institutions? And, if they pursue the former, how do they prevent dialogue with, say, the IMF and the World Bank leading to their incorporation?

The bankruptcy of the Third Way is not, therefore, equivalent to the death of social democracy. As long as capitalism continues to generate injustice and instability, movements seeking its reform will emerge to challenge it. In my view, however, these movements will still face the classical difficulties inherent in reformism. In particular, as I have already argued, the imperatives of capitalist reproduction set limits to what any reformist movement can achieve. Confronted with these limits, the movement will have to choose between abandoning its attempt to achieve a fairer and more humane world or seeking the removal of the system itself. Pursuing the latter option once again poses the question of agency. It requires the development of a mass movement centred on the organized working class that seeks the democratic reconstruction of society. Only in this way can the centres of concentrated capitalist power in the economy and the state be effectively challenged.[4]

It is the tragedy of social democracy, however, that usually it is the first option that is taken. The disillusionment caused by reformist governments' surrender to capital has helped to create the context in which first the New Right and the Third Way could force through neo-liberal policies. But history is not a prison. There is no reason why the past need endlessly repeat itself. The anti-capitalist movement that began at Seattle is creating the conditions in which a new left can emerge. Through seeking a democratic transformation of society, in which the mass of people develop the political forms required for them to take control of their lives and begin to address the problems of the planet, this left could offer a genuine alternative to the dead-end into which the Third Way leads.

Notes

Introduction

1   Although, according to Oskar Lafontaine, the slogan was coined by a much more traditional social-democratic figure, Willy Brandt, in 1972: see *The Heart Beats on the Left* (Cambridge, 2000), p. 42.

2   'Remarks by the President on Social Security', 9 February 1998, www.whitehouse.gov, p. 2.

3   A. Giddens, *The Third Way* (Cambridge, 1998), ch. 1.

4   A. Davidson, 'The Natty Professor', *The Business* (*Financial Times* Business Magazine), 11 March 2000.

5   A. Giddens, *The Third Way and Its Critics* (Cambridge, 2000), pp. 32–3.

6   J. Habermas, 'The European Nation-State and the Pressures of Globalization', *New Left Review*, I (235), 1999, p. 54.

7   N. Bobbio, *Left and Right* (Cambridge, 1996), p. 107 n. 6.

8   J. R. MacDonald, *Syndicalism* (London, 1912), pp. 68–9. I am indebted for this reference to David Stack.

9   P. Drucker, *Max Shachtman and His Left* (Atlantic Highlands, NJ, 1994).

10   P. Sedgewick, 'Varieties of Socialist Thought', in B. Crick and W. A. Robson, eds, *Protest and Discontent* (Harmondsworth, 1970), p. 37.

11 See C. Harman, *The Fire Last Time* (London, 1988).

12 Giddens, *Third Way*, pp. 2–3.

13 K. Marx and F. Engels, *Collected Works*, XXIV (London, 1989), p. 94.

14 Giddens, *Third Way*, pp. 4–5.

15 Ibid., p. 15.

16 P. Anderson, 'Renewals', *New Left Review*, II (1), 2000, p. 11.

17 Giddens, *Third Way and Its Critics*, p. 34.

18 G. Brown, 'Labour Party Conference Speech, Brighton', 25 September 2000, www.labour.org.uk, p. 6.

19 'Europe: The Third Way/*Die Neue Mitte* – Tony Blair and Gerhard Schröder', 8 June 1999, www.labour.org.uk, p. 1.

20 See also A. Carling, 'New Labour's Polity', *Imprints*, 3, 1999, and A. Callinicos, *Equality* (Cambridge, 2000), esp. chs 3 and 4.

21 Giddens, *Third Way and Its Critics*, p. 31.

22 'Intervention du Premier ministre aux Journées parlementaires du Groupe socialiste', 27 September 1999, www.premier-ministre.gouv.fr, p. 8.

23 'Discours de M. Lionel Jospin, Premier ministre, devant le Congrès de l'Internationale socialiste', 8 November 1999, www.premier-ministre.gouv.fr, p. 6.

24 See especially A. Rawnsley, *Servants of the People* (London, 2000) and D. Macintyre, *Mandelson and the Making of New Labour* (rev. edn, London, 2000).

25 It has been published as an appendix to B. Hombach, *The Politics of the New Centre* (Cambridge, 2000).

26 See A. Callinicos and M. Simons, *The Great Strike* (London, 1985).

27 T. Blair, 'Values and the Power of Community', speech to the Global Ethics Foundation, Tübingen University, 30 June 2000, www.number-10.gov.uk, p. 4.

28 J. C. Isaac, 'Intellectuals, Marxism and Politics', *New Left Review*, II (2), 2000, p. 11. See also A. Callinicos, 'Impossible Anti-Capitalism?', ibid.

Chapter 1 Masters of the Universe

1 Anonymous (J. Klein), *Primary Colors* (London, 1996), pp. 161–2.

2   D. Held, A. G. McGrew, D. Goldblatt and J. Perraton, *Global Transformations* (Cambridge, 1999), p. 2.

3   *Financial Times*, 22 and 23 May 1995.

4   T. Blair, 'Values and the Power of Community', speech to the Global Ethics Foundation, Tübingen University, 30 June 2000, www.number-10.gov.uk, p. 3.

5   A. Giddens, *Runaway World* (London, 1999), pp. 12, 13.

6   Ibid., pp. 8–9.

7   See, for example, A. Callinicos, *Against Postmodernism* (Cambridge, 1989), pp. 132–44; W. Hutton, 'Myth That Sets the World to Right', *Guardian*, 12 June 1995; 'The Myth of the Powerless State', *The Economist*, 7 October 1995; M. Mann, 'As the Twentieth Century Ages', *New Left Review*, I (214), 1995; M. Wolf, 'The Global Economy Myth', *Financial Times*, 13 February 1996; P. Hirst and G. Thompson, *Globalization in Question* (Cambridge, 1996); C. Harman, 'Globalization: A Critique of a New Orthodoxy', *International Socialism*, 2 (73), 1996; L. Weiss, *The Myth of the Powerless State* (Cambridge, 1998); K. N. Waltz, 'Globalization and American Power', *The National Interest*, 59, 2000.

8   N. Harris, *The End of the Third World* (London, 1986); F. Jameson, *Postmodernism, or the Cultural Logic of Late Capitalism* (London, 1991); P. Anderson, *The Origins of Postmodernity* (London, 1998).

9   Held et al., *Global Transformations*, p. 2.

10   Ibid., p. 16.

11   Ibid., p. 414.

12   See J. K. Galbraith's classic study, *The Great Crash 1929* (London, 1979).

13   Held et al., *Global Transformations*, p. 7.

14   A comparable argument, also relying on data provided by Angus Maddison, was made by Martin Wolf in 'The Need to Look to the Long Term', *Financial Times*, 16 November 1987.

15   Hirst and Thompson, *Globalization in Question*, esp. chs 2–4.

16   Held et al., *Global Transformations*, pp. 219, 260; see generally ibid., chs 3–5.

17   Harman, 'Globalization', p. 9.

18   Ibid., pp. 9–14.

19   M. Castells, *The Rise of the Network Society* (*The Infor-

mation Age, Vol. 1, 2nd edn, Oxford, 2000), pp. 135, 137, 147. Linda Weiss uses comparative studies of several major economies in order to highlight the contemporary role of the state as an economic actor: see *The Myth of the Powerless State*. Her account of 'governed interdependence' between the state and capital is, however, weakened by this concept's equivocal status: it seems to function simultaneously as an analytical model and a policy proposal.

20   K. Polanyi, *The Great Transformation* (Boston, 1957).

21   B. Woodward, *The Agenda* (New York, 1994), p. 84.

22   Ibid., p. 165.

23   C. Hitchens, *No One Left To Lie To* (London, 1999), p. 81.

24   R. R. Reich, *Locked in the Cabinet* (New York, 1998), p. 341.

25   R. Pollin, 'Anatomy of Clintonomics', *New Left Review*, II (3), 2000, pp. 17–18.

26   Castells, *Rise of the Network Society*, p. 140. Peter Gowan interprets these and other policies as aspects of a coherent strategy to maintain global US economic leadership: see *The Global Gamble* (London, 1999), ch. 5.

27   In contradiction to this interpretation, Christopher Hitchens argues that '[i]t wouldn't be fair to say that Clinton did all this [i.e. implemented Republican policies] after reluctantly discovering the limits of power,' *Mother Jones*, September/October 2000, but the scenes of frustrated rage described by Woodward seem well attested.

28   H. Wilson, *The Labour Government: a Personal Record* (Harmondsworth, 1974), p. 65. See also Ben Pimlott's account in *Harold Wilson* (London, 1993), ch. 16.

29   *Financial Times*, 13 March 1999. For Lafontaine's account of his departure, see *The Heart Beats on the Left* (Cambridge, 2000), esp. ch. 16.

30   Blair, 'Values and the Power of Community', p. 2.

31   Leadbeater in fact seeks to distance himself from the formula of the Third Way: see *Living on Thin Air* (London, 2000), p. 17. Nevertheless, the thrust of his argument that it is now possible to reconcile capitalism and social justice is at the heart of Third Way thinking.

32   Ibid., pp. 228, 167, 18.

33   Ibid., p. 41.

34   Castells, *Rise of the Network Society*, p. 69.

35 Leadbeater, *Living on Thin Air*, p. 114. George Monbiot describes a striking example of this process – the corporate penetration of scientific research in Britain: see *Captive State* (London, 2000), ch. 9.

36 Leadbeater, *Living on Thin Air*, pp. 167, 230, 235, 241.

37 Ibid., pp. ix, 61.

38 Ibid., pp. 220, 1.

39 Castells, *Rise of the Network Society*, p. 502.

40 Ibid., pp. 14, 16. On the basic concepts of historical materialism, see esp. G. A. Cohen, *Karl Marx's Theory of History* (Oxford, 1978), and A. Callinicos, *Making History* (Cambridge, 1987), ch. 2.

41 Castells, *Rise of the Network Society*, p. 17.

42 Ibid., p. 19.

43 R. Brenner, 'The Social Basis of Economic Development', in J. Roemer, ed., *Analytical Marxism* (Cambridge, 1986).

44 This argument is too narrow in the sense that it ignores the fact that technological innovation is often driven by military rather than economic competition. This points to more general weaknesses in Brenner's historical theory that I have discussed elsewhere: see *Theories and Narratives* (Cambridge, 1995), pp. 128–40. But these considerations do not invalidate my criticisms of Castells above.

45 Castells, *Rise of the Network Society*, p. 94. If anything this statement is too strong: the search for higher productivity and improved competitiveness may *motivate* technological innovation, but they do not *determine* what, if any, increase in productivity is actually generated by this innovation. The rate of productivity growth depends on many different factors irreducible to the desires of capitalists.

46 Ibid., p. 25.

47 See Callinicos, *Against Postmodernism*, pp. 121–7.

48 Castells, *Rise of the Network Society*, p. 60.

49 Ibid., pp. 180, 187.

50 Ibid., pp. 208, 210.

51 Ibid., p. 209.

52 *Financial Times*, 4 October 2000.

53 Castells, *Rise of the Network Society*, pp. 369–70.

54 R. Tomkins, 'Dotcoms Devoured', *Financial Times*, 23 October 2000.

55 Castells, *Rise of the Network Society*, pp. 29, 151.

56 Quoted in R. J. Gordon, 'Has the "New Economy" Rendered the Productivity Slowdown Obsolete?', 14 June 1999, www.econ.northwestern.edu, p. 2.

57 Castells, *Rise of the Network Society*, p. 92; see generally ibid., pp. 80–94. There is a useful survey of the debate on the 'New Economy' in a series of articles written by Gerald Baker in the *Financial Times* between 13 and 20 December 1999.

58 Gordon, 'Has the "New Economy" Rendered the Productivity Slowdown Obsolete?', *passim*.

59 Idem, 'Does the New Economy Measure Up to the Great Inventions of the Past?', 1 May 2000, www.econ.northwestern.edu.

60 R. Brenner, 'Uneven Development and the Long Downturn', *New Left Review*, I (229), 1998. The very extensive critical discussion of Brenner's article by Marxist economists and philosophers – see especially *Historical Materialism*, 4 and 5, (1999) – has not challenged his basic thesis of a crisis of profitability.

61 Martin's and Godley's analysis is developed in two jointly authored Phillips & Drew research papers, 'America and the World Economy' (December 1998) and 'America's New Era' (October 1999), in a presentation by Martin, 'America's New Era Revisited' (13 April 2000), and in an article by Godley, 'What If They Start Saving Again?', *London Review of Books*, 6 July 2000.

62 S. Brittan, 'Nonsense on Stilts', *Financial Times*, 13 May 1999.

Chapter 2 Guardians of Morals

1 S. Žižek, 'Attempts to Escape the Logic of Capitalism', *London Review of Books*, 28 October 1999, p. 7.

2 'Remarks by the President and Other Participants in Democratic Leadership Forum The Third Way: Progressive Governance for the Twenty First Century', 25 April 1999, www.whitehouse.gov, pp. 26–7.

3 Ibid., p. 5.

4 T. Blair, 'The Conservative Party Seems Neither to Understand Nor to Act Upon the Concept of Duty', *The Spectator*, 25 March 1995, p. 18.

5 Idem, 'Values and the Power of Community', speech to the

Global Ethics Foundation, Tübingen University, 30 June 2000, www.number-10.gov.uk, p. 4. It is a matter of fine judgement to assess the part played by religious faith in New Labour thinking. Blair and various of his ministers have ostentatiously (and no doubt sincerely) paraded their Christianity. But there are other kinds of Christian socialism – for example, the variant championed by that embodiment of the Old Left, Tony Benn.

6 N. Bobbio, *Left and Right* (Cambridge, 1996), p. 82.
7 I discuss the issues covered in this section at much greater length and (I hope) more depth in *Equality* (Cambridge, 2000).
8 A. Giddens, *The Third Way and Its Critics* (Cambridge, 2000), pp. 85, 120.
9 See Callinicos, *Equality*, pp. 52–79, and for much subtle discussion of the distinction between circumstances and choice, G. A. Cohen, 'The Currency of Egalitarian Justice', *Ethics*, 99, 1989; J. Roemer, *Theories of Distributive Justice* (Cambridge, MA, 1996); and R. Dworkin, *Sovereign Virtue* (Cambridge, MA, 2000).
10 S. White, 'What Do Egalitarians Want?', in J. Franklin, ed., *Equality* (London, 1997), pp. 70–1.
11 G. Brown, 'My Vision of a Fairer Britain for Everyone', *Times*, 3 June 2000.
12 'Remarks by the President and Other Participants in Democratic Leadership Forum', p. 17.
13 G. Brown, 'The Politics of Potential', in D. Miliband, ed., *Reinventing the Left* (Cambridge, 1994), p. 116.
14 Idem, 'The Conditions for Full Employment', Mais Lecture by the Chancellor of the Exchequer, 19 October 1999, www.hm-treasury.gov.uk.
15 See, for example, S. Brittan, *How to End the 'Monetarist' Controversy* (London, 1982).
16 'Lecture by the Chancellor of the Exchequer to the Royal Economic Society', 13 July 2000, www.hm-treasury.gov.uk, p. 8.
17 Letter to H. D. Henderson, 28 May 1936, in *The Collected Writings of John Maynard Keynes*, XXIX (ed. D. Moggridge; London/Cambridge, 1979), p. 222.
18 N. Lawson (1984), 'The British Experiment', quoted in idem, *The View from No. 11* (London, 1992), pp. 414–15. See, for

a rather less elegant restatement, Brown, 'Conditions for Full Employment', p. 5.

19 The evolution of Lawson's policy can be traced in *The View from No. 11*, esp. chs 7, 8, 33, 36, 69, 78 and 81. A detailed defence of Brown's version of this policy is offered by HM Treasury, 'The New Monetary Policy Framework', 19 October 1999, www.hm-treasury.gov.uk.

20 'Lecture by the Chancellor of the Exchequer to the Royal Economic Society', p. 8.

21 Callinicos, *Equality*, pp. 88–104.

22 Quoted, *Guardian*, 7 September 2000. A similar picture emerges from the government-commissioned studies whose findings are reported in *Persistent Poverty and Lifetime Inequality: the Evidence*, CASEreport 5/HM Treasury Occasional Paper No. 10, March 1999.

23 A. Giddens, *The Third Way* (Cambridge, 1998), p. 110.

24 HM Treasury, *Tackling Poverty and Extending Opportunity*, March 1999, p. 32.

25 G. Hodgson, 'The Big Boys', *Guardian*, 3 June 2000.

26 *Financial Times*, 27 May 2000; *Guardian*, 5 June 2000.

27 R. H. Tawney, *Equality* (4th edn, London, 1952), p. 157.

28 *Financial Times*, 13 April 2000.

29 *Guardian*, 14 July 2000.

30 *Financial Times*, 11 September 2000.

31 See, for example, 'Speech by the Chancellor of the Exchequer to the CBI Conference', 1 November 1999, www.hm-treasury.gov.uk, p. 4.

32 J. Plender, 'Raider of Company Cashflow', *Financial Times*, 31 October 2000.

33 P. Stephens, 'A Chancellor Writing a Cheque for Change', ibid., 19 July 2000.

34 S. Brittan, 'Fat Years After the Lean Years', ibid., 20 July 2000.

35 W. B. Gallie, *Philosophy and the Historical Understanding* (London, 1964), p. 158; see generally ibid., ch. 8. Gallie says that essentially contested concepts must be '*appraisive*' (ibid., p. 161), a term with a wider extension than 'normative', but the complications introduced by the broader term are not germane to the issues addressed here.

36 A. Carling, 'New Labour's Polity', *Imprints*, 3, 1999, and 'What Do Socialists Want?', in M. Cowling and P. Reynolds,

eds, *Marxism, the Millennium and Beyond* (Houndmills, 2000).

37 *Guardian*, 17 July 2000.

38 Blair, 'The Conservative Party', p. 18.

39 Giddens, *Third Way and Its Critics*, p. 49.

40 R. Dworkin, 'Rights as Trumps', in J. Waldron, ed., *Theories of Rights* (Oxford, 1984), pp. 153, 166.

41 I do not claim, of course, that victims and their families have no rights: as the Stephen Lawrence affair underlined, they have, for example, the right to a prompt and efficient investigation of the case. But all too often appeal to victims' rights is simply a cover beneath which barbarous and retributive conceptions of punishment are reinstated.

42 T. W. Adorno, *Negative Dialectics* (London, 1973), p. 3.

43 D. Selbourne, *The Principle of Duty* (London, 1994), pp. 3, 20.

44 Giddens, *Third Way and Its Critics*, p. 52.

45 Selbourne, *Principle of Duty*, p. 33.

46 J. Raz, *The Morality of Freedom* (Oxford, 1986), pp. 166, 167.

47 Ibid., p. 181.

48 See J. Rawls, *Political Liberalism* (extended edn, New York, 1996). Raz defines a rights-based morality as 'a moral theory the fundamental principles of which state that certain individuals have certain rights', *The Morality of Freedom*, pp. 193–4. Formally this definition fits Rawls, but it doesn't really seem correct to describe such a theory as 'rights-*based*' since, as I have already noted, rights are, in Rawls' theory, derived from his principles of justice. Raz claims that such theories have too restrictive a view of morality – for example, 'rights-based moralities cannot allow intrinsic moral value to virtue and the pursuit of excellence,' ibid., pp. 195–6. This may be a valid criticism of a theory such as Rawls', but, even if correct, it does not justify calling his theory 'rights-based'.

49 Raz, *Morality of Freedom*, pp. 205, 199. Given the commitment of socialists to the ideal of autonomy and of some contemporary liberals to that of community – see, for example, W. Kymlicka, *Liberalism, Community, and Culture* (Oxford, 1989) – it might seem that socialists and left-liberals (who, like them, would also treat equality and democracy as

of intrinsic value) share the same values. G. A. Cohen argues that

> [l]iberals do not believe that capitalism is a system of exploitation which should be overthrown in favour of a socialist society which is both possible and desirable. I believe all that, which certainly distinguishes my normative commitments from liberals', but I don't think that, in order to believe that, I have to believe any norms that liberals disbelieve. You have to distinguish between lack of distinctiveness at the level of fundamental norms and lack of distinctiveness at the level of embraced normative commitments. ('Self-Ownership, History and Socialism', *Imprints*, 1, 1996, p. 13)

Alternatively, one might say that the socialist challenge to egalitarian liberals is that their values are inconsistent with the requirements of capitalist reproduction and therefore can only be achieved in a socialist society: see, for example, A. E. Levine, *Arguing for Socialism* (London, 1984).

50 S. Hall, 'The Great Moving Right Show' (1979), reprinted in idem and M. Jacques, eds, *The Politics of Thatcherism* (London, 1983).

51 A. Gamble, 'The Free Economy and the Strong State', in R. Miliband and J. Saville, eds, *The Socialist Register 1979* (London, 1979). These formulations were rightly criticized for, among other things, underplaying the extent of economic interventionism under the Tories, but they are still useful as a way of capturing the principal ideological rationalization for Thatcherite policies.

52 G. A. Cohen, *If You're an Egalitarian, How Come You're So Rich?* (Cambridge, MA, 2000), pp. 120, 128; see generally ibid., chs 8–10, and idem, 'Incentives, Inequality, and Community', in G. B. Peterson, ed., *The Tanner Lectures on Human Values*, XIII (Salt Lake City, 1992).

53 G. A. Cohen, *Self-Ownership, Freedom, and Equality* (Cambridge, 1995), ch. 11.

54 See A. MacIntyre, *After Virtue* (London, 1981) and *Whose Justice? Which Rationality?* (London, 1989).

55 'Speech by the Chancellor of the Exchequer to the CBI Conference', p. 4.

56 See G. Monbiot, *Captive State* (London, 2000).

57 Quoted in A. Rawnsley, *Servants of the People* (London, 2000), p. 309.
58 S. Žižek, *The Art of the Ridiculous Sublime* (Seattle, 2000), p. 32.
59 Quoted in Rawnsley, *Servants of the People*, p. 105. See ibid., ch. 6, for the most detailed account to date of this sordid affair.
60 Žižek, *Art of the Ridiculous Sublime*, p. 33.
61 C. Leadbeater, *Living on Thin Air* (London, 2000), p. 15.
62 Giddens, *Third Way*, p. 15. See also idem, *The Consequences of Modernity* (Cambridge, 1990), and *Runaway World* (London, 1999), ch. 3.

Chapter 3 Saviours of Humankind

1 J. G. Ballard, *Super-Cannes* (London, 2000), p. 89.
2 T. Blair, 'We Are Fighting for a New Internationalism', *Newsweek*, 19 April 1999.
3 T. Blair, 'Doctrine of the International Community', speech to the Economic Club of Chicago, 22 April 1999, www.fco.gov.uk, pp. 2, 3, 4.
4 Ibid., p. 9.
5 'PM's Statement on the Suspension of NATO Air Strikes against Yugoslavia', 10 June 1999, www.fco.gov.uk, p. 4.
6 Blair, 'Doctrine of the International Community', p. 9.
7 Much more extended versions of the criticisms outlined in this and the following paragraphs will be found in N. Chomsky, *The New Military Humanism* (London, 1999), L. German, ed., *The Balkans, Nationalism and Imperialism* (London, 1999), and T. Ali, ed., *Masters of the Universe?* (London, 2000).
8 'Remarks by the President to AFSCME Biennial Convention', 23 March 1999, www.whitehouse.gov, p. 3.
9 J. Sweeney, 'Why Can't They See?', *Observer*, 30 May 1999.
10 J. Steele, 'Serb Killings "Exaggerated" by West', *Guardian*, 18 August 2000.
11 House of Commons Select Committee on Defence, *Fourteenth Report*, 23 October 2000, www.parliament.the-stationery-office.co.uk, para. 299.
12 'Remarks by the President to AFSCME Biennial Convention', p. 3 (emphasis added). This speech provides the starting point

of Peter Gowan's exhaustive analysis, 'The Euro-Atlantic Origins of NATO's Attack on Yugoslavia', in Ali, ed., *Masters of the Universe?*

13 The role of Peter Castenfeldt, a Swedish financier linked to the Russian government, who worked closely with senior German officials to broker the deal, was revealed in the *Financial Times*, 14 June 1999.

14 E. N. Luttwak, 'No-Score War', *Times Literary Supplement*, 14 July 2000.

15 A. Giddens, *The Third Way* (Cambridge, 1998), p. 70.

16 Idem, *Runaway World* (London, 1999), p. 18.

17 J. Rawls, *The Law of Peoples* (Cambridge, MA, 1999), *passim*; quotations from pp. 37–8, 93 n. 6. Rawls also mentions a fifth kind of society, benevolent despotism (ibid., p. 92), but it plays little part in his argument.

18 Ibid., pp. 48–9.

19 See, for example, ibid., pp. 117–18, where Rawls distinguishes between the circumstances in which societies find themselves and the choices that they make faced with these circumstances. This is one of the passages in Rawls' *oeuvre* that present an apparent inconsistency with his critique of desert in *A Theory of Justice*, where he argues that the choices individuals make necessarily reflect circumstances – such as the distribution of natural talents – over which they have no control. I am grateful to Matt Matravers for discussion of this point.

20 Rawls, *The Law of Peoples*, pp. 52–3, 79. For a brief critical survey of the now extensive debate over whether democracies will ever fight one another, see S. M. Walt, 'Never Say Never', *Foreign Affairs*, January/February 1999.

21 D. Held, A. G. McGrew, D. Goldblatt and J. Perraton, *Global Transformations* (Cambridge, 1999), pp. 443–4.

22 In their remarkable new book *Empire* (Cambridge, MA, 2000), Michael Hardt and Antonio Negri offer a far-left variant of this analysis. They argue that economic and cultural globalization is accompanied by the emergence of a new form of political sovereignty, Empire, which is irreducible to the domination of any specific imperialist state, even the US. Characterized by the absence of any boundaries to its dominion, Empire (as its name suggests) is most closely paralleled by the political order of ancient Rome. But, where Held,

McGrew and their co-authors put a positive spin on this development, Hardt and Negri see Empire as the latest form of capitalist domination, brought into being by workers' and anti-colonial struggles and in a permanent condition of crisis thanks to its dependence on the transnational 'multitude' whose creative energies it parasitically exploits. Brilliant though Hardt's and Negri's analysis often is, it is nevertheless vulnerable to the same fundamental objection that faces left-liberal theories of 'political globalization': as I seek to show in this chapter, there is no evidence that the development of multilateral political forms that allow the leading capitalist states to co-ordinate their policies and negotiate their differences is bringing about the disappearance of major conflicts of interest among the Great Powers or of the relative predominance of the United States among these powers. At most we see the emergence of a hybrid form of sovereignty in which the pursuit of nationally constituted interests is legitimized through appeal to transnational institutions (for example, the UN, NATO and EU) and the values they affirm; thus, as Hardt and Negri observe, humanitarian interventions assert 'a *right of the police*' that 'is legitimated by universal values' (ibid., p. 18).

23 Held et al., *Global Transformations*, p. 43; see also table 1.1, ibid., pp. 44–5.

24 Ibid., p. 425.

25 Ibid., p. 426.

26 R. O. Keohane, *After Hegemony* (Princeton, 1984), p. 31. For a *marxisant* version of this theory, which results in a cyclical philosophy of history, see G. Arrighi, *The Long Twentieth Century* (London, 1994).

27 R. O. Keohane, ed., *Neorealism and Its Critics* (New York, 1986).

28 See, for example, R. G. Gilpin, *War and Change in World Politics* (Cambridge, 1981).

29 C. Kindleberger, *The World in Depression 1929–1939* (Harmondsworth, 1987).

30 Keohane, *After Hegemony*, p. 135.

31 See N. I. Bukharin, *Imperialism and World Economy* (London, 1972), and A. Callinicos, 'Marxism and Imperialism Today', in Callinicos et al., *Marxism and the New Imperialism* (London, 1994). Held et al. cite the latter text but do not

appear to have understood its argument: see *Global Transformations*, pp. 3, 6.

32 Keohane, *After Hegemony*, pp. 136–7.

33 R. Brenner, 'Uneven Development and the Long Downturn', *New Left Review*, I, (229), 1998, ch. 2.

34 See F. Block, *The Origins of International Economic Disorder* (Berkeley and Los Angeles, 1977).

35 R. Brenner, 'Uneven Development and the Long Downturn', pp. 197–204.

36 G. Achcar, 'The Strategic Triad: USA, Russia, China', in Ali, ed., *Masters of the Universe*, p. 106.

37 J. S. Nye, Jr, *Bound to Lead* (New York, 1991).

38 Z. Brzezinski, *The Grand Chessboard: American Primacy and Its Geostrategic Imperatives* (New York, 1997), p. 59.

39 Ibid., p. 46. Brzezinski places Ukraine first in his list of 'critically important geopolitical pivots' of US strategy in Eurasia: ibid., p. 41.

40 Stratfor, 'Finally, NATO Tests a Resurgent Russia – in Kiev', 2 March 2000, www.stratfor.com.

41 For critical discussions of NATO expansion, see J. Rees, 'NATO and the New Imperialism', in German, ed., *The Balkans*, and G. Achcar, 'Rasputin Plays at Chess: How the West Blundered into a New Cold War', in Ali, ed., *Masters of the Universe?*

42 Held et al., *Global Transformations*, ch. 2.

43 *Financial Times*, 9 February 1998.

44 See R. Wade and F. Veneroso, 'The Asian Crisis: The High Debt Model versus the Wall Street–Treasury–IMF Complex', *New Left Review*, I (228), 1998, and P. Gowan, *The Global Gamble* (London, 1999), ch. 6.

45 See, for example, S. George, 'À Seattle, le commerce avant les libertés', *Le Monde diplomatique*, November 1999, and W. Bello, 'Reforming the WTO is the Wrong Agenda', in K. Danaher and R. Burbach, eds, *Globalize This!* (Monroe, ME, 2000).

46 A. Sinai, 'Le Jour où le Sud se rebiffa', *Le Monde diplomatique*, January 2000.

47 See D. Johnstone, 'Humanitarian War: Making the Crime Fit the Punishment', in Ali, ed., *Masters of the Universe?*, pp. 161–4.

48 Brzezinski, *The Grand Chessboard*, p. 10.

49 Ibid., p. 59.
50 Ibid., p. 198.
51 M. Wight, *International Theory* (London, 1991), p. 210.
52 See, for example, Gilpin, *War and Change in World Politics*, p. 29. Nye offers some useful criticisms of excessively mechanical theories of hegemony: see *Bound to Lead*, part I. On the limits of power in pre-modern empires, see M. Mann, *The Sources of Social Power*, I (Cambridge, 1986), ch. 5.
53 See the more nuanced discussions in Keohane, *After Hegemony*, ch. 3, and G. Achcar, 'D'un siècle américain à l'autre: entre hégémonie et domination', *Actuel Marx*, 27, 2000.
54 P. Anderson, 'Renewals', *New Left Review*, II (1), 2000, p. 12.
55 Stratfor, 'The Putin Doctrine: Nuclear Threats and Russia's Place in the World', 17 January 2000, www.stratfor.com, p. 2.
56 *Financial Times*, 24 June 2000.
57 Achcar, 'The Strategic Triad', *passim*.
58 'Stratfor's Decade Forecast: 2000–2010: A New Era in a Traditional World', 20 December 1999, www.stratfor.com, pp. 2, 3.
59 Stratfor, 'Why It's Not a New Cold War: Secondary Powers and the New Geopolitics', 6 March 2000, www.stratfor.com, p. 1.
60 'Stratfor's Decade Forecast', p. 4.
61 Stratfor, 'Why It's Not a New Cold War', p. 6.
62 For an important critique of Realism, see J. Rosenberg, *The Empire of Civil Society* (London, 1994).
63 Quoted Wight, *International Theory*, p. 134.
64 A. de Waal, *Famine Crimes* (London, 1997).
65 Johnstone, 'Humanitarian War', p. 150.
66 See, in addition to ibid., pp. 164–5, A. Callinicos, 'The Ideology of Humanitarian Intervention', in Ali, ed., *Masters of the Universe?* During the 2000 US presidential election George W. Bush and his advisers attacked the policy of humanitarian intervention defended by Al Gore and the outgoing Clinton administration. According to Stratfor, the row represented

the beginnings of a deep debate over foreign policy. On the one side, there are those who see the end of great power rivalry and view the military as a tool for policing minor regional unrest. On the other side are those who see the past ten years as a mere interregnum between great power rivalries and think the armed forces should be preparing for major wars. ('A Last a Foreign Policy Issue: Bush, Gore and the Balkans', 23 October 2000, www.stratfor.com, pp. 5–6.

But if the Bush administration does hold the latter view, it does not follow that it will, as many pro-Democrat commentators have predicted, retreat into isolationism. Objective pressures – both the global nature of US interests and the difficulty of achieving significant domestic policy changes in a grid-locked Congress – tend to push American presidents towards an activist foreign policy. It should be remembered that during the 1992 election campaign Bill Clinton promised to focus on domestic issues: his first foreign intervention – the disastrous Somalian adventure – was inherited from his predecessor, George Bush Sr. The ideology of humanitarian intervention is too useful a policy tool to be lightly abandoned.

67 Johnstone, 'Humanitarian War', pp. 164–5.
68 'Building "a Bridge of Understanding" between Russia and the West: Edited Transcript of Press Conference Given by the Prime Minister, Tony Blair, and the Russian President-Elect, Vladimir Putin, Foreign and Commonwealth Office, London', 17 April 2000, www.fco.gov.uk, p. 2.
69 Brzezinski, *The Grand Chessboard*, pp. 42, 43.

Chapter 4 Alternatives

1 For analyses of the East Asian and Russian crashes and their consequences, see A. Callinicos, 'World Capitalism at the Abyss', *International Socialism*, 2 (81), 1998, and P. Gowan, *The Global Gamble* (London, 1999), ch. 6.
2 A. Giddens, *The Third Way and Its Critics* (Cambridge, 2000), pp. 37, 126, 127, 129; see also idem, *The Third Way* (Cambridge, 1998), pp. 150–1.
3 J. Habermas, 'The European Nation-State and the Pressures of Globalization', *New Left Review*, I (235), 1999, p. 54.
4 See O. Lafontaine, *The Heart Beats on the Left* (Cambridge, 2000), esp. ch. 15.
5 Habermas, 'European Nation-State', p. 58.

6 Idem, 'Bestialität und Humanität: Ein Krieg an der Grenze zwischen Recht und Moral', *Die Zeit*, 29 April 1999, online edition (www.ZEIT.de), p. 2.

7 J. Stiglitz, 'The Insider', *The New Republic*, 17 April 2000, online edition (www.thenewrepublic.com), p. 1.

8 Ibid., p. 8.

9 T. Blair, 'Doctrine of the International Community', speech to the Economic Club of Chicago, 22 April 1999, www.fco.gov.uk, p. 6.

10 Giddens, *Third Way and Its Critics*, pp. 125–6.

11 J. Plender, 'Western Crony Capitalism', *Financial Times*, 3 October 1998.

12 *Financial Times*, 25 October 2000.

13 R. Dworkin, *Sovereign Virtue* (Cambridge, MA, 2000), p. 351.

14 *Financial Times*, 27 January 1995.

15 J. M. Keynes, *The General Theory of Employment Interest and Money* (London, 1970), p. 159.

16 If, indeed, any changes of any substance take place at all. Reporting on the third meeting of the Financial Stability Forum (FSF) set up after the 1997–8 crisis, the *Financial Times* (24 March 2000) suggested that the process of financial reform had stalled: 'observers of the process note that the immediate spur to reform – continued chaos in the world's financial markets – is absent. And with the industrialized G-7 group of countries, let alone emerging market nations, at odds over how far the process of regulation should go, the FSF faces a difficult time.'

17 *Financial Times*, 25 November 1999.

18 Ibid., 30 June 2000.

19 Quoted in M. Wolf, 'The Big Lie of Global Inequality', ibid., 9 February 2000.

20 *Independent*, 30 November 1999.

21 M. Wolf, 'Banking for the World's Poor', *Financial Times*, 21 June 2000.

22 M. Lundberg and B. Milanovic, 'The Truth about Global Inequality', ibid., 25 February 2000.

23 Ibid., 21 September 2000.

24 Quoted in C. Harman, *The IMF, Globalization and Resistance* (London, 2000), p. 6.

25 *Financial Times*, 24 December 1999.

26 M. Castells, *The Rise of the Network Society* (*The Information Age, Vol. 1*; 2nd edn, Oxford, 2000), p. 145.

27 Giddens, *Third Way*, p. 151.

28 P. Anderson, 'Renewals', *New Left Review*, II, (1), 2000, p. 11. See p. 7 above.

29 J. Lloyd, 'The Trial of José Bové', *Financial Times*, 1 July 2000.

30 See, for example, P. Bourdieu, *Acts of Resistance* (Cambridge, 1998), S. George, *The Lugano Report* (London, 1999) and G. Monbiot, *Captive State* (London, 2000). For a critical intellectual survey of the new movement, see C. Harman, 'Anti-Capitalism: Theory and Practice', *International Socialism*, 2 (88), 2000.

31 D. Held, A. G. McGrew, D. Goldblatt and J. Perraton, *Global Transformations* (Cambridge, 1999), p. 236.

32 Ibid., pp. 236–7.

33 For up-to-date figures that indicate a slight tendency for foreign direct investment to become more widely diffused, see ibid., pp. 248–51.

34 S. George, 'À Seattle, le commerce avant les libertés', *Le Monde diplomatique*, November 1999.

35 Monbiot, *Captive State*, ch. 10.

36 H. Kaufman, 'Big is Bad for Global Prosperity', *Financial Times*, 28 July 2000.

37 Considered as a structure of competitive accumulation, modern capitalism is best understood (following Bukharin's path-breaking analysis during the First World War) as embracing both market competition and the geopolitical rivalries constitutive of the international state system: see A. Callinicos, *Theories and Narratives* (Cambridge, 1995), pp. 128–40, and 'Periodizing Capitalism and Analysing Imperialism' in R. Albritton, M. Itoh, R. Westra and A. Zuege, eds, *Phases of Capitalist Development* (London, forthcoming in 2001).

38 See, for a much more extensive analysis, C. Harman, 'The State and Capitalism Today', *International Socialism*, 2 (51), 1991.

39 Castells, *Rise of the Network Society*, p. 276 n. 93, 468, 470.

40 See especially A. Giddens, *A Contemporary Critique of Historical Materialism* (London, 1981). For Marxist responses see E. O. Wright, 'Giddens's Critique of Marxism', *New Left Review*, I (138), 1983, and A. Callinicos, 'Anthony

Giddens: A Contemporary Critique', *Theory & Society*, 14, 1985.

41 ' "The greenhouse gas trading market, though only embryonic, is expected to become one of the largest commodity markets in the world," says Cantor Fitzgerald, a financial services company involved in emissions trading,' *Financial Times*, 18 November 2000.

42 For far more on capitalism and the environment, see P. McGarr, 'Why Green is Red', *Internationalism Socialism*, 2 (88), 2000. One obstacle to this convergence of Red and Green is the widely held belief that Marxism is insensitive to environmental questions. Indeed, G. A. Cohen accuses Marx of relying on a 'technological fix' – unlimited abundance made possible by the endless expansion of the productive forces – to ensure that communism would be a conflict-free society: *Self-Ownership, Freedom, and Equality* (Cambridge, 1995), ch. 5. In an important new book, John Bellamy Foster throws down a root-and-branch challenge to such interpretations, arguing that humankind's relationship with nature is one of the leading themes of Marx's thought from the very start of his intellectual career, and that one of his major concerns in *Capital* is the evidence – derived especially from Liebig's chemical researches – of the destructive effect that capitalist agriculture was having on the soil: *Marx's Ecology* (New York, 2000).

43 See also A. Callinicos, 'Social Theory Put to the Test of Politics: Pierre Bourdieu and Anthony Giddens', *New Left Review*, I (236), 1999, pp. 85–95, and *Equality* (Cambridge, 2000), pp. 113–14.

Afterword

1 Ronald Dworkin is an example of this tendency: he describes his theory of equality of resources as a 'third way' between 'old egalitarians' who ignore 'personal responsibility' and conservatives who ignore 'collective responsibility': *Sovereign Virtue* (Cambridge, MA, 2000), p. 7. But, since he describes the 1996 Welfare Reform Act – signed into law by Bill Clinton – as 'a plain defeat for social justice' (ibid., p. 320). Dworkin's third way is clearly not the same as the Blair–Clinton Third Way.

2 Sir S. Cripps, 'Can Socialism Come by Constitutional Methods?', in C. Addison et al., *Problems of Socialist Government* (London, 1933).

3 Boris Kagarlitsky's *Recasting Marxism* (3 vols, London, 1999–2000) is perhaps best seen as an attempt to develop such a strategy.

4 This project is considerably elaborated in A. Callinicos, *The Revenge of History* (Cambridge, 1991), ch. 4.

Index